D1282481

I consider David Drury to be a   ar. I've
turned to him for counsel many times. In *Transforming Presence*, David helps us
feel what it was like to actually be with Jesus and how it can change everything.
Now many readers can discover what I already have: David Drury is a gift to the
kingdom of God.

—MAX LUCADO, pastor and best-selling author

David Drury is creative, thoughtful, and wise. In a world of people seeking God,
here is wisdom for finding the path.

—JOHN ORTBERG, senior pastor at Menlo Park Church, author of
All The Places to Go and *The Life You've Always Wanted*

You will *not* sit down and read this in one sitting! The transforming presence of
Jesus himself will stop you. You will reflect, rejoice, review, and renew. Jesus
comes alive in twenty-first-century life on every page. I have found that David
Drury not only writes about Jesus, but humbly seeks to live like Jesus every day.

—JO ANNE LYON, general superintendent, The Wesleyan Church

I've grown to appreciate my friend David Drury and his passion for Jesus. In
Transforming Presence, David reminds us that being like Jesus means knowing
the Jesus of Scripture—to be transformed in and by his presence!

—ED STETZER, executive director, LifeWay Research

Creative, imaginative, and compassionate—David Drury takes us to meet Jesus
when we need him most in the pages of *Transforming Presence*.

—LEITH ANDERSON, president, National Association of Evangelicals

Have you ever felt overworked, exhausted, or trapped? We too often search
aimlessly for encounters that enhance our networks and feed our ambitions but
have proved lacking. Our dear friend David Drury has, with refreshing insight,
reminded us of what is most deeply satisfying: the transforming presence of Jesus.
David invites us to encounter Jesus anew. *Transforming Presence* renewed our
hearts with the hope that encountering Jesus again and again makes all things new.

—GABRIEL AND JEANETTE SALGUERO, cofounders of
National Latino Evangelical Coalition, copastors of The Lamb's Church, NY

In this book, David Drury puts his finger on the most significant ingredient leading
to life change, and the very element most of us miss as Christ-followers. Our problem
usually isn't a lack of content. It's lack of presence. *His* presence. *Transforming
Presence* takes us on a journey so that we, like the followers of the early church,
can actually experience Jesus. It's our greatest need—not more information but
transformation. I highly recommend this book.

—TIM ELMORE, president, GrowingLeaders.com

I don't know anyone I admire more than David Drury. When he speaks, I listen. When he writes, I read. Without a doubt, this book will bless you.

—JOHNNIE MOORE, president, The KAIROS Company;
senior contributing editor, *The Christian Post*

In *Transforming Presence*, David Drury pours out the kind of discerned wisdom that can only come from years of learning, unlearning, and relearning the ways of Jesus in the world of human struggle. If you're feeling exhausted, unsatisfied, trapped, powerless, stuck, overwhelmed, afraid, guilty, marginalized, or grieved, then prepare for breakthrough—this book is for you.

—J. D. WALT, sower-in-chief, Seedbed Publishing

Life is fun until reality shows up. Life is a wonderful gift, but it can be difficult at times. David Drury delivers honest stories with biblical foundations that will guide you in the good times and encourage you when you encounter life's speed bumps, curve balls, and unexpected challenges.

—DAN REILAND, executive pastor, 12Stone Church, Lawrenceville, GA

David leads us through the winding alleyways of faith and religion, beyond the conundrums and contradictions, and the frenetic pace of life. He invites us to encounter God and to live a life that invites others to do the same. I commend to you to take this journey. It will change you!

—STEPHAN BAUMAN, president and CEO of World Relief

Children look for, sometimes even cry for, someone rather than something. For me, hearing, "Daddy's home!" is pretty awesome. It's refreshing and life-giving to be the object of a child's admiration. In Scripture, *childlike* was a word that Jesus used often and with high regard because we also need Someone not something to make our lives better. David Drury points us back to those life-giving cries of our own souls in his new book *Transforming Presence*. And I imagine Jesus thinks it's pretty awesome to answer our calls today.

—TODD BURPO, author of *Heaven Is for Real*

David Drury masterfully takes us into the encounters of real people in history who met Christ and his transforming power. These stories give us massive hope for our real lives, emotions, and challenges today. Seeing what Jesus did in the past helps us know what he can still do in our present situations—so this book is a manual for your hope in God, no matter what you are going through.

—MATT BROWN, evangelist, author of *Awakening*, founder of Think Eternity

Transforming Presence

How Being with Jesus Changes Everything

David Drury

wesleyan
PUBLISHING HOUSE
wphstore.com

Copyright © 2016 by David Drury
Published by Wesleyan Publishing House
Indianapolis, Indiana 46250
Printed in the United States of America
ISBN: 978-0-89827-982-5
ISBN (e-book): 978-0-89827-983-2

Library of Congress Cataloging-in-Publication Data

Drury, David (Chief of Staff)
Transforming presence : how being with Jesus changes everything / David Drury.
    pages cm
Includes bibliographical references.
ISBN 978-0-89827-982-5 (pbk.)
1. Bible. John--Criticism, interpretation, etc. I. Title.
BS2615.52.D78 2016
226.5'06--dc23

                               2015030481

Cover design: Cody Rayn

CONTENTS

For downloadable resources, visit
wphresources.com/transformingpresence.
A group study DVD is also available.

ACKNOWLEDGEMENTS

I t was not until my seventh book manuscript that I typed the word *acknowledgements* accurately, but just now I typed it wrong again so there goes the streak. For that reason and many more I must acknowledge that I need help. The acknowledgements in a book are about gratitude and thanks, but another meaning of the word is the "acceptance of the truth or existence of facts." So some of this is more than gratitude; it's just *fact*. The *truth* is, I couldn't have if these wouldn't have—

If Dave Ward, Amanda Drury, and Russ Gunsalus wouldn't have dreamed with me early on, I couldn't have been so creative.

If John Drury and Zach Aument wouldn't have offered deep biblical and theological insight, I couldn't have escaped the shallows.

If Kyle Ray wouldn't have asked such probing questions, I couldn't have understood what a pastor and a church need most from a book like this.

If the team at Wesleyan Publishing House wouldn't have been so patient and collaborative, I couldn't have gotten this project off the ground.

If Indiana Wesleyan's Jackson Library and Spring Hill Camps wouldn't have provided such great places to write, I couldn't have gained the uninterrupted focus required.

If so many wouldn't have graciously allowed me to present these ideas in messages to them, I couldn't have sharpened them for you to read in final form. These include the wonderful people of Kingswood University; Southern Wesleyan University; the Missional Holiness Conference; the Korean Evangelical Holiness Churches; Wesleyan churches; Nazarene churches; and the European, Turkic, and Arabic Mission Conference.

If Gloria, Natalie, and Candace wouldn't have organized my workweek so expertly, I couldn't have had the energy to write on nights and weekends.

If those I work for (Jo Anne and Max) wouldn't have mentored me so generously, I couldn't have written with confidence.

If Maxim, Karina, and Lauren wouldn't have cheered on a dad who spends a good deal of time typing, I couldn't have written at all because they are more important than this.

And as usual, if my wife, Kathy, wouldn't have believed in my writing so much, I couldn't have believed you'd want to read these words in the first place.

INTRODUCTION

Do you read the Bible in an attempt to be more like Jesus by looking at things from his perspective? If so, that's a good objective. Some say it's the whole point of reading the Bible. The only problem is that it's sometimes hard to relate to Jesus' point of view. He is the Son of God after all, and reading the Bible this way just makes you work ever harder to be like Jesus. When you fail, you become discouraged. That's when Scripture reading becomes a shame-inducing task, yet another part of life that makes you feel worse about yourself. That is certainly *not* the point of reading the Bible.

There is another way to read the Bible—or at least another way to read the Gospels. Instead of reading Matthew, Mark, Luke, and John through the eyes of Jesus, try reading them through the eyes of the people who encountered the transforming presence of Jesus. Put yourself in their shoes as we walk through the first half of the book of John. I am praying your reading of the Bible will change in at least three ways because of this.

THEY FELT WHAT YOU FEEL

First, you'll find that the people mentioned in Scripture had feelings similar to yours. Their situations were real and hard, perhaps even harder than your own. They can inspire you to overcome the challenges you face. Each chapter in this book is given a title that describes the situation of a person encountering Jesus. These words capture the feelings and circumstances of each person. There are words like *overwhelmed*, *grieved*, and *stuck*. A few more are *exhausted*, *guilty*, and *trapped*. Others are *powerless*, *afraid*, *unsatisfied*, and *marginalized*. Do any of these words describe you now? Have they described you in the past? Will they in the future?

In these pages, I will often ask, "Have you been with Jesus?" Each time that question comes up, think of the ways you've felt like the people in these stories in the past, right now, or when you may in the future. In those situations, did you intentionally look to discover the transforming presence of Jesus already with you? As you read the Bible, try putting yourself in the shoes of those who have been with Jesus, and if the shoe fits, then the Bible will come alive for you with newfound intensity, and your attitude and understanding will begin to change.

AN ENCOUNTER WITH JESUS CHANGES EVERYTHING

Second, by putting yourself in the shoes of the people who met Jesus, you'll see how a single encounter with the transforming presence of Jesus changed the trajectory of their lives. They each felt that their circumstances had painted them into a corner. The key for them was not merely to better understand their circumstances. They didn't need to process what they had gone through, blame someone else, or empower themselves. No, what they needed most was to be with Jesus Christ. He really was present. And his presence is transforming. We forget that. God became human to be with us. Unbelievers struggle to come to grips with the concept that a man was God. But believers often have the opposite problem. They struggle to realize that the God they believe in became fully man. As John put it: "The Word became flesh and made his dwelling among us. We have seen his glory, the glory of the one and only Son, who came from the Father, full of grace and truth" (John 1:14). One of my favorite thinkers once said, "The Word became flesh, then we spend most of our time turning him back into words again." Please understand that what matters is not the words I've written here. What matters is that the Word himself—Jesus, the transforming presence—can change everything for you.

When he comes along, the possibilities shift. The future is restored. Everything changes. I hope you want this and will find it in your own transforming encounter with Jesus.

MORE LIKE JESUS

Third, reading the Gospels through the eyes of those who encountered Jesus is a surer path to becoming like Jesus. You'll never become more like Jesus by trying harder. You do that by being with Jesus. If you rely on anything other than the transforming presence of Jesus to make you more like him, it won't work. Each of those who encountered Jesus' presence as recorded in the book of John had already tried hard at life. Most of them were quite religious. Some had committed their entire lives to seeking God. But an encounter with Jesus right where they were led them to become like him.

JESUS SHOWS UP

Let's launch into the first half of the book of John together. There you'll see ten situations in which someone struggled in life, but everything changed when they experienced Jesus' transforming presence.

Often Jesus is right there in front of us, but we are unaware of it because we are not looking for him. Jesus might be *with you*, but you aren't *with him*; you haven't noticed him. That was true for each of the ten we will meet. In fact, nearly every person in the Gospels did not recognize the presence of the Son of God right away. Yet once they did recognize him, everything changed. Recognize Jesus as being with you, and his transforming presence will change everything.

You may think you already recognize his presence, figuring that's a part of your belief system: "Jesus is everywhere—I feel his presence." You may think you notice not only when he shows up, but also when he's provided for you.

Are you sure you haven't failed to recognize his presence from time to time? Even *most* of the time? And if you really are with Jesus, why hasn't everything changed? These are legitimate questions for you whether you've just begun to follow Christ of have been doing so for decades. Remember that even some who followed Jesus for years failed to recognize his transforming presence. In fact, that's where John began his book about Jesus: "He was in the world, and though the world was made through him, the world did not recognize him. He came to that which was his own, but his own did not receive him" (John 1:10–11).

Let's start in John 2, at a party where Jesus showed up but his transforming presence went unnoticed.

1

EXHAUSTED

JOHN 2:1–11

Jesus loves parties. The gospel of John makes that clear about our Lord from the start. The loudest gathering with the most music was where you'd most likely find him. Yes, he escaped to quiet places to pray while everyone else slept; but when the party hats came out, the band started to play, and the drinks flowed freely, you might be surprised to find that Jesus was there in the middle of it all.

This is good to know of our Savior, because our religious establishments can be somewhat stiff, and we might think Jesus would feel out of place at a party, perhaps longing to escape to a seminary library. But Jesus was entirely comfortable participating in parties, and most of the books at a seminary library are about him anyway. What's more, Jesus didn't choose the associations others might like. He knew that being *with* people is the only way to influence them. He didn't behave like everyone he associated with, but he was *with them* in spite of their behavior. His frequent attendance at parties with unsavory characters earned him the moniker "friend of sinners." He was as much at home at a block party as the monastery. Jesus shows up to listen to sermons and participate in prayer meetings, but he is also the kind of Savior that shows up to birthday celebrations, bachelor parties, and bar mitzvahs.

Don't assume parties aren't spiritual occasions. Jesus' first public miracle was at a wedding party—the miracle wouldn't have happened had the bride and groom not invited him. What if you invited Jesus to your big game, friendly cookout, or a sweet sixteen party? How could this change the direction of the festivities? If you do choose to invite him, keep your eye to the crowd. If you notice his presence, ask him to participate as only he can. Who knows—he might even work a subtle miracle without the guests ever knowing. The presence of Jesus changes everything when you are exhausted; he has resources you know nothing about.

A MOTHER NOTICES

Before any member of my family heads out the door in the morning, they have to pass an informal security check with my wife, Kathy. She looks each of us over like a customs agent and observes things we must correct before leaving. "Lauren, you need to brush the back of your hair—not just the sides, and you need socks on." The inspection continues. "Karina, you need to wear tennis shoes because it's gym day, remember?" The family Transportation Security Agent turns to the oldest child. "Max, you need to switch into shorts because it's going to be over eighty degrees today." The husband is last to face scrutiny. "Dave, you must have cut yourself shaving, you have a paper dot on your face. Oh, and I'm not sure that shirt fits anymore." After a few changes, we come back for a final check before our brave family heads out into the world, prepared.

Mothers notice what others miss.

Mary, the mother of our Lord, did. She was invited to a party after a wedding; it may even have been one of her friends or relatives who gave their child in marriage. Mary was attentive to how things were going in the party, noticing the decorations that were attractively "just so." Earlier she had noted the garb of the betrothed in the wedding itself, smiling at the intricate designs on the young woman's dress. The reception was going well too—the entertainment was perfect, the food was plentiful, the wine. Wait a second . . . the wine!

Mary saw the servants looking fretful in the hallway. "These people sure have been drinking a lot of wine today." Mary continued to observe the crowd. "Why is that maître d' waving an older servant to the back?" Suddenly the servants stop returning to refill cups. "That table over there has been calling for refills for several minutes with no service." This mother noticed what others missed.

Mary excused herself quietly and headed for the kitchen. There she startled a circle of servants, who looked up at her with a tinge of worry in their eyes.

"What's going on here?"

The older waiter blurted out the truth: "They drank too much. The family only paid for a few hours' worth, and the guests have stayed far beyond. Many more were invited than we were told. We just poured our last pitchers."

The observant mother considered her friend's family. She knew they were not wealthy; but a wedding is a once-in-a-lifetime occurrence. "Not being able to entertain guests at this reception would be a massive embarrassment. Everyone will know of the bride's parents' financial situation. They will be humiliated."

"Wait here," Mary commanded.

Not being of wealth herself, her options were limited. She didn't have the means to pick up the extra tab. "But he could do something. I have no doubt he will have compassion on them." She walked briskly to a table where her Son sat listening to stories with the friends that seemed to follow him around everywhere these days.

The one called Andrew was delivering the punch line to a joke. His big brother laughed so hard he nearly choked on his bread. James and John slapped Andrew on the back and hooted. "As I recall, those are the fishermen who are called 'the Sons of Thunder.' How ridiculous."

She stopped at the foot of the table, locking eyes with her Son at the head, who had been watching her approach. She had been thinking over what she would say. "But those eyes. It's always those eyes."

She caught herself slipping back to long-held secret memories of gifts from foreign dignitaries and visits from angelic beings, of strange dreams and stranger visions, of the smell of straw mixed with the sight of blood.

She knew every curl of his hair, each freckle on his shoulders. She remembered how hot he liked his tea and how he used to kick one foot out from the blanket to stay cool at night. "He did that at the age of three. He still does it now at thirty. But I never could really tell what this one was thinking." Whenever she caught his gaze, it would freeze her, as it did now. "But I always knew what he would do. Unlike the other kids, I could always count on him to do the right thing."

It was odd at first, seeing him tempted by a special treat for dinner on the table when he didn't know she was looking. He would go and look at it and even smell it, but not take. Later, when he was a teenager, she could see when things made him angry, but he would let it pass and a calm would come over him. This was true unless he encountered an injustice. He would not let injustice pass; his anger would remain and he would do whatever it took to make things right.

He never spoke back to her, not once. By the time he became a man, it was downright supernatural. "In every way, he was like every other boy. Except this: he was perfect." He was perfect, never doing anything wrong; he was normal, but perfectly normal.

The silence brought her back to the party, still staring at those eyes. Yet it was different now, like staring into the night sky, not into the eyes of the One she used to nurse by the fire. She noticed Jesus' friends frozen silent as well, staring at her, waiting for her to snap out of it.

Self-conscious, she blushed. "Come speak with me, Son." Jesus followed her to a corner, where she bent her head to intimate a secret: "They have no more wine" (John 2:3). She went from speaking to the floor to looking up at her boy. "No, he's a man now. Taller even than Joseph was, his . . . father."

Jesus broke her gaze and looked out at the crowd. Taking a bite of the bread he had carried from the table, he studied the situation. He swallowed and kept looking. Without glancing back to her, he said, "Why do you involve me?" (v. 4).

Mary looked up at her Son for a long moment. When he finally returned her gaze, she raised an eyebrow and bobbed her head as if to say, "You know why."

He suppressed a chuckle by taking another bite of the bread. Looking off to the clouds in the distance, and with a cheek still full of bread, he said, "My hour has not yet come" (v. 4). Jesus brushed crumbs off hands, his robe, and then his beard. Patting his mother on the shoulder, he walked back to his table. Peter was telling a well-rehearsed fishing story.

Mary walked back to the kitchens, where the servants waited expectantly. She pulled them toward the door and pointed across the room to her Son. "The tall one over there in the white and green wool. 'Do whatever he tells you'" (v. 5). And thus the stage was set for the beginning of the public ministry of Jesus.

GOD'S CALENDAR

Why did John begin the account of Jesus' ministry with a wedding? More to the point, why did Jesus choose to launch his ministry at a wedding? John merely recorded that the redemptive plan of God was ushered in at this event.

It is encouraging to know that Jesus had a plan for his ministry. He had an "hour" already in mind (v. 4). He had a timetable. God seems to have strategically timed the redemptive arc of history.

Yet it can be frustrating to think that we are left guessing at what God's plan is, regardless of our situation. That causes us to wonder why we should pray at all, to ask him for anything, if he has everything planned in detail anyway.

This story shows us how it really works. There *was* a plan. There *was* an hour. The Father and the Son had been mulling it over for some time. Maybe it would begin with healing a lame man on the Sabbath; that would make a point. Or a blind man in the Jerusalem temple; boy, that would turn some heads. He could kick things off with a long sermon and lay out his whole vision for the future in one take. Or he could start on a high note and raise someone from the dead; that would sort of speak for itself and be a good way to start, revealing the end in the beginning.

But here's the amazing thing Jesus did at this wedding: he truncated his timetable. The Son of Man rolled out the strategic plan ahead of schedule.

Why? Because a young couple was in need, that's why. That's it.

The presence of Jesus changed things for this couple; he has resources they knew nothing about.

Somehow the One who spun the sun, earth, and moon into their circles and established our days and nights changed his plan on the fly. The One who measured out the seasons our calendars are measured by, yes, the great Calendar-Maker himself, adjusted his calendar—for us! The One who created everything was willing to reschedule his debut for a couple of locals getting hitched in the backwater town of Cana.

Here's the point this passage is making: the Word was willing to go with the flow in unveiling his redemptive plan because of a few empty wineglasses and a potentially embarrassed bride. Jesus was willing to push up the date of his opening night because someone was in need. The Light himself adjusts in light of your circumstances.

WHATEVER HE SAYS

Peter's face was red with the anticipation of the climax of his story: "So Andrew gets a look at the fish and says, 'Let's keep the size of this one to ourselves for once.'"

Jesus listened without laughing along as he normally would; he'd heard the punch line many times anyway. As the group whooped it up, Jesus walked to the kitchen, where the servants were still waiting, empty pitchers in hand.

With no other options and wanting to avoid the clatter of empty cups at the reception, the servants followed Jesus' instructions to the last detail, their obedience complete and specific. They filled all the massive ceremonial washing pots with water, right up to the brim. This would have totaled 120 to 180 gallons of water, weighing about fifteen hundred pounds. That's roughly the load capacity of a Ford F-150 pickup. After completing the task, sweaty from the work, they turned to the man for the next step. "Serve," he said, waving his arm toward the pots, then turning on his heel and returning to his table.

The servants were stunned. They exchanged puzzled looks. Already groaning at the stares they would get when they tried to serve water instead of wine, they realized this was going to be a long night. Then an older servant remembered the woman's instructions: "Whatever he says."

He dipped a pitcher into the pot and pulled it up full. He looked inside. It was dark. Odd. He grabbed a cup and poured. The water flowed out red. He drank. His eyes doubled in size with each gulp. He began to laugh as the other servants grabbed cups of their own and drank and laughed in joy. The group of dour servants who had been ready to skip town had become a bunch of giddy children at this unexpected delight.

Just then the master of ceremonies burst into the kitchen, finding each servant holding a cup of wine, laughing and drinking. He shouted, "What are you doing in here in your cups while your guests have empty ones? Get out there, do your jobs, and serve the wine!"

The servants were all too happy to do so. As everyone received their refill and the spirit of the party began to rise, several got up to dance to a new tune played by the musicians. The master of ceremonies was served a new cup. This man must have been a master vintner, for he knew this wine was beyond anything else he'd tasted. He pointed to the parents of the bride at the honored seats, saying, "At most weddings they bring out the cheaper wine when the guests are drunk, but now you bring out the best wine!" Lifting his cup high, he shouted, "Give a cheer for the bride and groom!"

All cheered, except Mary. She was watching the room. She first saw the father and mother of the bride looking at each other, wondering what was happening. They shrugged their shoulders and moved to the middle of the room for a dance.

It is astonishing that Jesus not only provided precisely at the point of their need, but also provided much more *quality* and *quantity* than required. The wine was so much better than needed, as the master of ceremonies pointed out in verse 10. You have to read between the lines on this one. Calculating with the volume of the jars in mind, Jesus created enough wine out of thin air to flow freely through *five* weddings. The lesson? Jesus provides what is *more* and *better* than you ever did, without you even knowing it.

Mary's six-year-old niece, Jesus' cousin, grasped a single finger on his much-larger hand and led him onto the dance floor. He responded by reaching out a formal hand toward her, and when she grabbed it, he picked her up to twirl her around to the music. The girl squealed in delight, and he joined his laughter with that of others, dancing awkwardly, as wedding guests do.

Mary allowed a smile to cross her face.

HAVE YOU BEEN WITH JESUS?

There's more to the wedding story if you read between the lines. Notice that nowhere does it say the bride and groom were worried about the wine. They were seated at the table of honor, enjoying themselves. They were the focus of celebration, but they had no clue that they were about to be humiliated. They didn't know that her father had nearly become the butt of a joke told at every wedding for a generation. And they didn't know that they had just been with the Son of God or that he had provided for them when they needed it most. They went on with their merry business, thanking people for gifts and dancing the night away. They never asked for help. They didn't even know how desperately they needed it.

Neither do you.

You think your resources will last forever. You are unaware that you are exhausting them. You don't realize how much you depend on God until the last pitcher is poured. Even then you don't think of it until you ask for another and none comes. You live as if your resources are unlimited, while only those in the background, only those who are most observant, can see that you are running on empty. Perhaps you're right there with the wedding couple, and you're about to run out even though you don't know it yet.

I had a nagging suspicion that things weren't as they should be in my life, but I didn't know for sure until a certain holiday, the first day of 2002. New Year's Eve should be full of friendship and parties and expectancy for a new year to come. New Year's Day should be full of rest, football, barbeques, and getting amped up for a year's worth of opportunity.

But that year our family did none of that. We were escaping a year we would rather forget and entering a year that held no prospect of change. My work was all consuming, and all too frustrating.

Instead of organizing a party, we reorganized a closet. My wife had a stack of bins on the floor, their contents strewn about the living room. We sorted items as we discussed our lives. The more we discussed things, the worse we felt. Have you ever had one of those conversations, where the longer it goes the worse life seems? There were no options on the table. We struggled in our relationship. We had few friends, and none of them knew how we were feeling. This fact made us feel even worse. I didn't feel that I was being a good father to our toddler son. Added to my frustrating work life, I felt like a complete and utter failure in all aspects of life.

I was always tired. More than tired, in fact. When you are tired, you can take a nap to recover, go to bed early, or sleep in. You can take a vacation. The weariness I felt was deeper than lack of sleep. I'd come back from a day off even more frustrated than before. A vacation day was just an empty day to stew on how bad things were.

I didn't understand it till later, but I had exhausted my resources. I had tried everything, tried to tap into any solution to restart my life and work and family, and nothing had worked. Every source of fuel I might try was an empty tank.

I sat amid the stacks of storage containers, stewing, venting, and exhausted. I'm not sure you would have seen it in me, but I was about to blow.

I yelled in anger—not at my wife but at my life. Yet she was the one present. Thankfully our toddler was napping upstairs. I strode across the room and hit the stack of empty containers with my hand, smashing them against the wall. Several of them, made of brittle plastic, shattered. I continued to vent, stomping into the garage to rage and growl, finally sitting down on the steps and crying in frustration.

My wife opened up the door just a crack, then came out and put a hand on my shoulder.

Have you been there? Have you been so frustrated with your life that you had nowhere to turn? Have you ever felt so exhausted by circumstances that you saw nothing left to do but scream at the ceiling? If you've been here, I bet even the memory is exhausting for you.

What followed that moment of rage was a sign that I was not alone on planet earth. My wife gave me grace (although I did wind up buying a few storage containers). My supervisor at work accepted my resignation that very day with grace. He also helped me find another job in his district so I would land on my feet. The church I went to work for loved on my family and me. That congregation continued to show us kindness even after we moved on to join the staff of a larger church, where we continued to heal and serve fruitfully for many years.

I didn't know I had exhausted my resources, but God did. He was already reordering events, moving the clock forward, and changing his plans to ensure I survived the lowest season of my life. I thought everything was over. But he was just getting started with me.

Exhaustion never schedules an appointment.

You don't see it coming. It doesn't send a text fifteen minutes before arrival. There are no social media notifications for burnout. When it arrives, you finally see that you need others, and that you truly need God.

JESUS WANTS TO MIRACULOUSLY PROVIDE FOR US

Thankfully, God is always ready to provide—it doesn't matter when. There is no "bad time" for God. You never ring him up only to hear, "Could you call back in fifteen minutes?" For those of us who have become attuned to the sustaining work of God, every day is a chance to have redemptive conversations because we have a Savior who once slipped into the pantry to turn water into wine—just to keep the party going. We know that any moment might be the redemptive moment. Jesus is always ready to lower a rope to those at the end of theirs.

What's more, he provides for us in miraculous ways, as he did at the wedding at Cana. Others help us pack and move, and they might slip us some cash. They may even go the extra mile and babysit our kids. However, God does things that only God can do, and we often fail to notice.

We aren't aware that he met our need any more than we knew we had the need in the first place. That's the scary thing about all this. We think we have it covered. We think, "Things aren't like I want them to be, but if I can just _____, it will turn out all right." You rarely fill that blank with anything spiritual, do you? You don't fill the blank with anything related to provision from heaven.

Instead, you write,

"Get a raise."

"Get engaged."

"Find a job."

"Move out of this town."

"Get a 3.75 GPA."

"Buy a new car."

Whatever it might be, it's some action you will do or some thing you will acquire. If you are honest with yourself, you'll admit that you never write "Rely on Christ" in the blank. Your plan is to provide for yourself.

You know better than that, though, don't you? You realize that you can't provide for yourself forever any more than you could spin a top perpetually. You couldn't throw a baseball around the earth and catch it coming round the other side; you know you can't sustain much at all. So what keeps you going?

God.

Thank him for it!

Perhaps you would thank him if you were aware of what he's done in the first place. Make a list. Make a long list of the things God provides for you. Start with the ability to read this book. Add the light you're reading it by (or the backlight on your device). Thank him for the room you're sitting in, the park bench, the beach, or the boat.

Jesus provides for you at all time, so it is right to praise his work at all times, thanking him for his unseen hand in transforming the world so you'll make it through. Like the wedding couple, you might be on the verge of embarrassment, financial ruin, or relational heartbreak and never know it. And Jesus is in the kitchen, changing your world's ordinary water questions into answers of the finest vintage you've ever tasted.

Sometimes only the servants know how the miracle came about. They were the only ones who saw it happen at the wedding at Cana. Only they, and Mary, knew what was up. They worked behind the scenes and saw events at their worst, and knew whom to point to when all ended well.

I've been in ministry since I was eighteen years old. As a pastor, I'm like one of the servants at this wedding. I've seen how bad things can get, and how God encounters people right there in the middle of it.

I've seen a medical doctor cry about her wayward children. I've seen an independently wealthy man pray deep prayers of dependence on God. I've seen "do it all" stay-at-home moms at the end of their ropes. I've seen someone with a PhD grow speechless when asked what the third grader for whom he serves as a volunteer mentor means in his life. We ordained servants of the kingdom see this stuff all the time. It's one of the only real perks of the job: seeing God's people encounter the tiny miracles of his grace when their own resources have run out.

Notice the transforming presence of Jesus today. Peer into the kitchens and back hallways to see how he is at work in the wedding of life. Through the rest of these pages, we will see over and over again how Jesus encounters people at a very low place on their map's topography. He shows up and everything changes. An encounter with the transforming presence of Christ can do that. Just one conversation. Just one touch. And it becomes the starting point for a new adventurous journey in life.

Pay close attention to the ways you lack the resources needed to live on your own. Admit that you can't pull it off going solo, and get ready to find a vibrant life in Christ that you never thought possible — a life that is "more than all we ask or imagine" (Eph. 3:20). The presence of Jesus changes everything when you are exhausted; his unlimited resources make this transformation possible.

PRAYER

You are with me, Jesus. Even when I do not notice what you are up to, I know you are present with me. I confess that, too often, I have assumed I could make things happen on my own, that I had the resources I needed to do what I chose. I am thankful that you have provided for me in unseen ways, and I rely on you constantly. Thank you, Jesus, my provider!

FOR REFLECTION

1. On what occasions do you suspect that God provided for your needs, though you didn't recognize it at the time? Can you name a time when you exhausted your resources but somehow made it through? What would it look like if you were to embrace a moment of gratefulness for his provision in the past, or be attentive to how he is providing for you right now?

2. At what other times in Scripture did Jesus show up and provide for someone when he or she was unaware of it?

3. Read Ephesians 3:14–21. What might it mean for Jesus to be so fully present with people that he would "dwell in [their] hearts" (v. 17)? Do you know someone who might be well described by the phrase "filled to the measure of all the fullness of God" (v. 19)? What is your "immeasurably more" (v. 20)?

4. In what specific ways do you need the transforming presence of Jesus to provide the resources you've exhausted this week or this month?

2

UNSATISFIED

JOHN 3:1–21

have made this one longer, only because I have not had leisure to make it shorter."[1] So wrote the seventeenth-century mathematician and philosopher Blaise Pascal. Indeed, it takes an immense amount of time to write something well, but briefly. Perhaps that's part of the reason we love Scripture so much. A single verse can capture so much meaning in so short a space.

It is a challenge to boil down an idea to just one sentence. However, when the British Empire attempted this almost 150 years ago, they pulled it off. Or at least they borrowed a line that pulled it off.

The English had extended their might around the world, returning with the spoils of trade and symbols of its colonial reach. One such symbol was from Egypt. The English had shipped a massive obelisk called Cleopatra's Needle from the Nile, through the Mediterranean, up the Atlantic coast, and into the Thames to plant it on English soil. On September 12, 1878, they raised the 3,500-year-old needle to the sky. It had once been a gift to an Egyptian pharaoh, now it was a gift to the English people. Pharaohs once rode past it in their chariots; now English kings sent out their dominating clipper ships under its shadow. Moses may have studied in the shade on its steps, but now Sir Arthur Conan Doyle could pen his volumes beneath it.

To mark this occasion, the British government sealed a message to future generations beneath this monument from the past. They placed a time capsule under the obelisk, which included symbols and messages of significance from their culture. Someday, city officials reasoned, when England goes the way of ancient Egypt, excavators will open the box to find a slice of Victorian England. The selections? A set of coins, children's toys, a city directory, photographs of the twelve most beautiful women of the day, and a razor.[2] An odd assortment to represent themselves to the future, I'd say.

However, along with these items, they included one sentence, which they thought would be the most important message to send into the future. It was the core of what they believed. The British translated this line into 215 languages to ensure that whatever future civilization might find it could read it. What message did the British send to the future? This one: "For God so loved the world that he gave his one and only Son, that whoever believes in him shall not perish but have eternal life."

What a choice! No sentence holds more in fewer words. Martin Luther called this verse "the heart of the Bible, the gospel in miniature." He noted that the genius of the verse is that it is so simple a child can understand it, but it packs the deep thoughts of redemption into just a few "pungent words."[3] When Billy Graham was asked by a TV reporter to state the basic message of his preaching, Graham quoted that verse and said, "I think that sums it up, which is known to almost everybody. . . . That's the sum total of what I preach."[4] Another preacher less well-known than Graham has called it "the greatest sentence ever written."

That sentence, of course, is found in John 3:16. The verse is so well-known that people seldom bother to recite it anymore. They just say, "Ya know, like John 3:16." At sporting events people hold up signs that read only "John 3:16." The reference itself has become a symbol, presumably because we instantly not only know what it says, but also what it means. The presence of Jesus changes everything for the unsatisfied because only he is able to satisfy our deepest needs.

FOR WHOM?

John 3:16 makes us think of someone who is far from God, someone who is part of *the world* that *God so loved*. We perhaps think of the irreligious, even the down and out. These are people who need God yet are unaware of how much he loves them. We want to tell them the good news of *eternal life* so they will not *perish*. And we know this is possible only if they meet the *one and only Son*, so that they can *believe in him* and leave their godless lives behind, follow his teachings, and be saved.

That is the message of John 3:16, right? It is a verse for the lost, an evangelistic verse, the best one of all. Its message is entirely familiar. We have heard John 3:16 more times than we've heard the national anthem. Surely we know what it means.

Except that we have missed a huge part of *whom* it is for.

John 3:16 falls, of course, in John chapter 3. But we often pull that verse out of context. In fact, it may be the most mis-contextualized verse in all of Scripture. What is the context? For that we need to go to Jerusalem, two thousand years ago, at night.

NICODEMUS

Wild-eyed, prophetic types seemed to emerge from the Dead Sea caves or northern hills or river valleys each spring. Nicodemus had seen messiahs come and go. He'd seen his fair share of parable-weaving rabbis teaching enthralled crowds in the countryside. A few even came from Galilee. For a people craving freedom from their oppressors, for those with apocalyptic visions and whose favorite book of the Bible was Isaiah, the time was always ripe for a new messiah to rise up and gather a following. Yet these messianic campaigns always ended, though perhaps not always in the same way. Some ended in violence, sparking a riot to be put down by the authorities and the execution of the recently rumored messiah. Some ended in a flash—suddenly gone, to other, unknown places. Some ended in the slow, pitiful decline of followers, until everyone could see what Nicodemus already knew: They were not the real deal. These so-called messiahs were pale imitations of the Immanuel of Isaiah 7. They were not the "lamb [led] to the slaughter" in Isaiah 53:7. They were shadow messiahs, bleating like prideful goats.

Now this One had appeared and was the first to make Nicodemus ask new questions. Other teachers didn't have the depth of this One. They said things to placate the crowds or incite them. "Messiahs" are people-pleasers. They might make bombastic, prophetic-sounding pronouncements, but they were never directed toward the people standing in front of them. They always gave a prophetic word "for them," not "to you."

But this One, he went after his own people. Nicodemus had edged his way into the temple courts to hear this man speak parables that confounded even Nicodemus's own wisdom. Usually the words of mock messiahs were like chaff that blew away with the breath of a single question. These pretenders never knew as much about the Holy Scriptures as Nicodemus did. Many people were asking him about this new One, from Podunk, Galilee. Nazareth, wherever that was.

However, this One didn't just teach scriptural wisdom with accuracy and truth; he also expounded upon those truths in ways that were practical, ingenious. After hearing those teachings, Nicodemus was left with questions of his own. While meditating on the Scriptures one morning, he recalled something this One from Galilee had said and he began reciting it to himself. Catching himself and feeling ashamed, he returned to reciting portions of Leviticus to correct his thinking.

Yet many people sought his opinion on this One, the One named Jesus. Clearly, the powerful wanted Nicodemus to work his magic, to find some flaw in the Teacher's platform and blast it to pieces. But he couldn't. What's more, he wouldn't. He had become entranced by the teachings and actions of this man. So this most religious of men, Nicodemus, made a decision. He would go to Jesus at night to ask some questions—not trick questions or subtle traps. He would ask open, honest questions in a sincere attempt to learn more about Jesus' teachings.

So in the context of the third chapter of John, verse 16 is meant first for Nicodemus, a very religious man. Surely it is also meant for us and for any reader of the book of John. But it starts with the context of a conversation with Nicodemus.

When you read John 3:16, you may think it is for the lost. You may think of it as a verse you read to someone who is far from God, someone who is irreligious, down and out, and needs Jesus in their life. Someone unlike you. You may want to put yourself in the shoes of Jesus, as the one sharing the truths to someone far from God. But in this story you are not Jesus.

You are Nicodemus.

You may protest and say, "This isn't meant for me. I'm already saved, for goodness' sake. I'm OK with God."

Surely that's what Nicodemus thought. He was the most "OK with God" person around. Even Jesus called him "Israel's teacher." If anyone was "in" with God, it was Nicodemus. So while you might think the words of John 3:16 are for the irreligious person, they were brought forward in a conversation with one of the most religious people around. Why is that?

The answer may bother you a bit. I know it bothered me when I first realized it.

What if the need to be "born again" applies not merely to people who are far from God joining the family for the first time? What if this new birth Jesus talked about is intended for all people, including people who are already religious?

What if those who have been born once into the family of God sometimes need a new birth, like Nicodemus did, to truly see the Spirit come alive in them?

What if John 3:16 is as much for believers who are nevertheless unsatisfied with their spiritual lives?

And if all of this might be true, what would it look like if religious people suddenly changed radically and were transformed to live out the gospel? That's worth thinking about.

HAVE YOU BEEN WITH JESUS?

Perhaps you are more like Nicodemus than you might think. You know how to go through most of the motions of Protestant Christianity. But like him, no matter how much you know about God, the church, and the Bible, you are a relatively unsatisfied religious person. You want more. You need to see how it all fits together. You don't want to deal with all the same old sins. You don't want to fight the same fights. You don't want to repeat the never-ending monotony of religion until the day you die. You don't like to think of yourself as "religious." But you're a pretty churchy person, right? You read Christian books (at least this one for a start). I suspect you're a relatively religious person and want new life in your spiritual life, just like Nicodemus did.

If you, like our Nick at Night, approached Jesus and tried to make affirming small talk, Jesus might reply in much the same way: "I tell you the truth, unless you are born again, you cannot see the Kingdom of God" (John 3:3 NLT).[5] You might be taken aback and think, "Jesus, why are you changing the subject so abruptly? I just paid you a compliment. And you immediately talk about this new birth concept, out of the blue?"

Jesus does this because "no one needed to tell him about human nature, for he knew what was in each person's heart" (2:25 NLT). Jesus doesn't need to do small talk with you any more than he did with Nicodemus. He knows what's in your heart. He knows you want more from your spiritual life, that you are unfulfilled.

After hearing of the new birth, Nicodemus questioned Jesus: "How can an old man go back into his mother's womb and be born again?" (3:4 NLT).

Jesus wasted no time in outlining the step an unsatisfied religious person like Nicodemus would need to take: "No one can enter the Kingdom of God without being born of water and the Spirit. Humans can reproduce only human life, but the Holy Spirit gives birth to spiritual life. So don't be surprised when I say, 'You must be born again.' The wind blows wherever it wants. Just as you can hear the wind but can't tell where it comes from or where it is going, so you can't explain how people are born of the Spirit" (vv. 3:5–8 NLT).

Perhaps because we know we're supposed to believe what we read in the Bible, these words don't mess with us like they should. Think about it for a moment. What if *you* went to talk to Jesus in the middle of the night and he told you that you need a rebirth in your spiritual life because the religious things you've been doing have no real spiritual value for you? What if he told you that you, yes *you* who have believed and accepted God's salvation, need to nevertheless be born again? You don't need to go to church more or read your Bible more or say your prayers more. All those things are fine and good, but they won't do what needs to be done. Jesus tells it straight to the sincerely and devoutly religious: You need to be born of the Spirit.

"How are these things possible?" Nicodemus asked (v. 9 NLT). And we would too, if Jesus had told us this.

"You are a respected Jewish teacher, and yet you don't understand these things?" Jesus replied to Nicodemus (v. 10 NLT).

What would Jesus say to you?

"You've been going to church since you were a baby, yet you don't understand these things?"

"You are a Sunday school teacher, and yet you don't understand these things?"

"You went to a Christian school, and yet you don't understand these things?"

"You read your devotions habitually, and yet you don't understand these things?"

"You have all those degrees, and yet you don't understand these things?"

"You have that position in the church, and yet you don't understand these things?"

"You were a part of that kids' club program when you were a child, with the outfit and all the badges for memorizing Scripture and doing good deeds, and yet you don't understand these things?" (OK, I'll admit it: this one is about me.)

Yes, this conversation with Nicodemus is sounding a whole lot more like the kind of conversation *you* might have with Jesus than one a completely irreligious and lost person might have. It seems Jesus wants you—yes, you—to be born again.

SNAKES IN NUMBERS

My wife hates snakes. Truly, nobody in my family likes them. But my wife's hatred of slithery serpents is vehement. Because of this, we all take perverse joy in pointing out snakes to her. At a zoo, the kids love to stand next to a snake tank until their mother comes by, just to witness her revulsion. When a snake appears on a television program, the kids pause, on that channel, and say, every so subtly, "Oh, look at that." Kathy takes the bait. She puts her hand to her mouth and shudders. The kids squeal in delight. Never one to withhold joy from my children, I purchased a realistic plastic snake, which they hide in locations for their mother to discover. To be honest, it has strained my marriage. My kids believe it has been worth it.

If you hate snakes, then the incident Jesus referred Nicodemus to next is the worst one in all the Bible. When the scriptwriter for *Indiana Jones and the Raiders of the Lost Ark* designed the snake-filled tomb for the ark discovery scene, he needed only to read Numbers 21 to get the picture right. And that is the place Jesus led Nicodemus next.

There we read the story of the Israelite people, unsatisfied and complaining to Moses in the desert. "The people grew impatient on the way; they spoke against God and against Moses, and said, 'Why have you brought us up out of Egypt to die in the wilderness? There is no bread! There is no water! And we detest this miserable food!'" (Num. 21:4–5).

By this point, God had it up to his omniscient eyeballs with the ungrateful Israelites. He allowed poisonous snakes to enter their camp. Curious young boys were bitten first. Then old women in their sleep. Soon something slithered around the bottom of every bedroll. The tents were overrun by snakes large and small. People were poisoned. People were dying.

The people's lack of faith and alienation from God (the heart of sin) caused them to be unsatisfied with all God had provided for them. Now their sin strangled them, and they couldn't survive—or sleep—without aid. Moses went to God and pleaded for a solution.

God gave one: "Make a snake and put it up on a pole; anyone who is bitten can look at it and live" (Num. 21:8).

Each poisoned boy or old woman, each and every Israelite who merely looked upon this symbol and trusted in God's aid would be saved. Those who could walk moved to the pathways between the tents. Those who could only crawl did the same. Those about to pass were carried by family and friends. A man held up his wife's head so she could peer to the distant bronze serpent on the pole. She did so and was healed. It took just one look, and something magical—supernatural—happened, something only God could do. Significantly, the people were satisfied only as their sin was overcome.

It is no wonder Jesus asked Nicodemus to recall this passage. It is a powerful illustration anticipating the crucifixion of Christ. The first half of the book of John sets up the last half. The first half, featured in this book in your hands, tells of the people whose lives were transformed by the teachings and miracles of Jesus. It shows that Jesus is the Son of God. The second half shows what the Son of God did to provide that transformation for all who might look upon him; he was raised up. Just as Moses raised up the bronze serpent in the desert, so the Son of God would be raised up; and each unsatisfied, sin-sick, snake-afflicted religious or unreligious person who looks upon him would experience something only God can do.

Only God can reach across and satisfy what is the origin of all sin—independence from him. As long as we are religiously busying ourselves about fixing our snake-bitten souls on our own (in our "flesh"), our yearnings remain unsatisfied. The only satisfaction for independence from God is dependence upon him. We can (we must) only look up.

So it's not just the beginning but the whole journey of transformation Jesus calls being "born again." You're saved. You're forgiven. I believe that. You've likely made some decision to cross a line of faith. You're a believer. But is your life being transformed by Jesus so that it is being made new? Is your life so different from before that someone might describe you as a new person? Are you experiencing new birth?

Nicodemus wasn't. He was as religious as they come. But it matters not how much you know. He could quote Scripture better than you, I bet. He could quote the first five books of the Bible from memory. Can you? I can't. But Jesus still called him to new birth.

I had to come to grips with the fact that I was a believer, I was a Christian, but I wasn't really being "born again." I had to admit that Christians have taken that term to be shorthand for "you're in." We've wanted to see "salvation" as merely a momentary occasion, rather than God's transforming work. We've acted as if we can merely say a prayer, receive forgiveness, and we're done—I'm now a "born again believer." After all, the purpose of a life is about so much more than its birth.

To be sure, God can transform a person's heart through a moment of honest confession and prayer. But it often doesn't happen so handily, especially among the very religious. I've had to admit something, and I'll confess it to you: I knew a lot about the Bible, but I wasn't being born again. I had a baptism certificate, but not a new-birth certificate. I had gone to Christian school and was later even an ordained minister of the gospel of Jesus Christ, and I still wasn't experiencing it. I confess

I was what we have so many of in the church today: an untransformed, unsatisfied, uninspired believer. In the truest sense of Jesus' meaning, I wasn't being born again.

Perhaps you think you are. But pause for a minute and ask yourself if you really, truly are. If you're hung up on the term *born again*, think "transformed life." Are you truly transformed? Or are you like me, like Nicodemus—unsatisfied and looking for more?

If so, Jesus offers you a new life. The Spirit will come into your heart and truly transform you.

FINDING WHAT I'M LOOKING FOR

I once visited a megachurch in a huge city and checked out their young adult service. This was an edgy experience, involving laser lights in place of candles and rock music in place of an organ. The preacher wore torn designer jeans and had spiky, bleach-tipped hair. There were funny videos and interesting announcements. It was a blast.

At one point, the band started a very familiar tune, even if it wasn't one I had heard in church before. A kid next to me, who must have been about nineteen, started to croon out the lyrics along with the singer: "I have run through the fields . . . only to be with you."[6] As the familiar song continued, almost everyone in the audience started to sing along, and at the chorus it seemed all two thousand people were belting out the same line, as if they were at a U2 concert: "But I still haven't found what I'm looking for."

All of us chanted this new-fangled creed of sorts. Acknowledging together that, with Bono, we believe these truths. Yet just as all churchy people must eventually admit to themselves, we confessed the truth: "I still haven't found what I'm looking for. . . ."

We haven't, have we? We haven't found a transformed life in regular church attendance. We haven't found new birth in our sporadic devotional lives. We aren't made new by yet another Christian book, including this one.

No, we still haven't found what we're looking for. Until that moment when we realize that though, like the Israelites, we might be in the family of God, we might be believers, but we aren't saved from the sting of sin. It poisons us. Like Nicodemus, we may know a lot about God, but we must admit that believing God exists hasn't made us born again. We must be "born of the Spirit," as Jesus said.

This is dangerous to admit to yourself. But it is essential. C. S. Lewis said it this way: "On the whole, God's love for us is a much safer subject to think about than our love for Him."[7]

When we think of John 3:16, we should focus on the love of God for us. That is critical. He does love us. He does save us. We believe in him. But he does so much more. Don't stay in the safe confines of reciting his love for us. Become the kind of person who loves God with all your heart, mind, and soul. Become the kind of person who loves others with the same outpouring of the Spirit. Be born again! Be transformed!

A TRANSFORMED LIFE

I've seen what a born again life looks like. Many times. I have seen it perhaps most clearly in Ross Hoffman.

Ross died in August 2013 as a middle-aged man with just one newborn grandkid. Perhaps because his life was cut tragically short, we took the time to step back and examine this remarkable man and consider what God had done in him.

Ross was known as a "good guy" and had done good things in life. But something happened to him at one point in his forties, and it was as if God had turned on the after-burners of his spiritual life. From that point on, Ross modeled what it means to be a personally invested lay member of a congregation. He mentored children, teens, and young adults. He served the church diligently behind the scenes as it worked to raise millions of dollars for a new ministry center. He then served again to redirect the church's energies not merely to fill up that new building, but also to use it as a giving and sending center with the aim of sending millions of dollars and hundreds of leaders beyond its walls. He influenced his church to be more and more an outpost in the kingdom of God, much more than a building.

Honestly, I have never seen a layperson influence a large church in such a powerful way in such a short time. He was tireless in trying to turn my attention, as a pastor, to things that matter to God but are often overlooked by the church. He was a model at "leading up" to help his pastors shift their church to become missional. While it appeared that we pastors were leading Ross, more often Ross was leading us.

Ross was in the habit of sending me Scriptures that he had read and thought would encourage me. He also emailed prayers for my specific ministry role. How he made the time for this is beyond me. His passion was matched by an unparalleled faithfulness, which is an especially powerful pairing of giftedness. The Holy Spirit had so transformed him that these kinds of deeds, which go beyond person-ality and temperament, were possible. It was almost as if Ross had been "born again" in midlife. He was saved before this, I'm sure of it. But now he was being transformed—he was finally living as a new person in Christ.

Ross had two grown children, Logan and Jolie. At the funeral, they read a letter that included these lines that pretty much sum it up: "Our dad would not have liked us saying this about him, but he was holy. He was never otherworldly, but he was a saint. Dad showed us what it meant to live a life worthy of the calling we have as Christians, how to see the unseen reality in people and situations and then to take action, always closing the gap between this world and the kingdom of heaven."[8]

You can have this new life that Ross had. Don't think that your position as a member of the family of God is the point here. "It doesn't matter whether we have been circumcised or not. What counts is whether we have been transformed into a new creation" (Gal. 6:15 NLT). Focus on what counts: your transformation. Instead of just believing in Jesus, let your life be entirely swallowed up in his. Then you will be "in Christ" and everything will be new. "Therefore, if anyone is in Christ, the new creation has come: The old has gone, the new is here!" (2 Cor. 5:17). By doing so, you can "count yourself dead to sin but alive to God in Christ Jesus" (Rom. 6:11).

Will you receive this new birth today? Jesus offers it to you and to all other religious types like Nicodemus. It isn't complicated. Look to Christ for this to happen. New birth doesn't come from this book. It doesn't come from a formula. I'm not even sure it comes from a prayer I would write on this page. It comes from Jesus *alone*. Look to him. Like the unsatisfied Israelites in the desert, look to what is lifted up before you in sacrifice. Look to the cross and say more than "Forgive me." Say, "Change me, satisfy my longings, make me new in you!"

Remember: The presence of Jesus changes everything for the unsatisfied because only he is able to satisfy our deepest needs.

But I have already said too much. Look to him and say what you need to say. Put down this book and have a little talk with Jesus. Then he will do in you what he wants to do.

And then later on, hopefully soon, people will look at your life, like I looked at Ross's life, and say, "You're like an entirely different person." May it be so.

PRAYER

You are with me, Jesus. I don't always understand what you're telling me, but I believe you are speaking. I admit that I'm not fully satisfied with my spiritual life. I need you to make my life new. I cannot do this myself. My efforts by themselves will mean nothing. I want to be made new in you, so that it's like being born again, again. Thank you, Jesus, my Savior!

FOR REFLECTION

1. In what ways are you more like Nicodemus than you might have thought in the past? Describe your level of satisfaction with your spiritual life. Where do you need the transforming presence to make things new?

2. Read John 3:1–21. In what ways did Jesus think Nicodemus needed everything to change in his life, even though he was religious?

3. Do you know people like Ross Hoffman, who lived a life truly transformed by the presence of Jesus Christ? How might you become more like such people, as they are more like Jesus? In what specific ways might you follow their example as they follow the example of Christ (1 Cor. 11:1)?

4. John 2:25 says, "No one needed to tell him about human nature, for he knew what was in each person's heart" (NLT). What is in your heart right now that you are unsatisfied with and want to affirm that Jesus already knows, so he might continue to change your nature?

3
TRAPPED

JOHN 4:1–42

The barn seemed enormous to us city kids, visiting from out of town. My cousin Josh and I had built a huge hay castle together with second, third, and fourth cousins we had met for the first time at this reunion. We ran about, panting and red-faced, deep into the night as our parents talked over hotdogs, brats, and carry-in food. We loved playing with the huge metal hooks, grabbing hay bales, and digging a deep hole into a stack several stories high. Our deep pit served no purpose other than to satisfy our curiosity. We wanted to see how deep we could go. We passed bales up and out of the pit. At one point, the kids at the top of the hay mound thought it would be fun to toss hay from the top onto those of us deep in the pit. As it rained hay, the light disappeared and some heavier clumps started to fall on our heads. Fear crept up the back of my neck like a threatened cat. I started to climb. I turned around to have Josh follow me and I saw that he was huddled in a corner, not moving at all and holding his chest.

He was trying to catch his breath, and I was freaking out a bit myself. We both felt trapped at the bottom of that hay hole. Only later did I discover that he was having the first asthma attack of his life. In that dark deep pit with hay falling on my head, I felt as if I couldn't breathe. Josh literally couldn't. He was suffocating. After much yelling and arguing with the kids at the top of the pile, we got Josh out of the pit, called for parents who immediately called an ambulance, and, thankfully, he recovered.

Recently I recalled this event with Josh's dad, my uncle. Though some thirty years have passed, he looked me dead cold in the eyes and said, "Yes, that was incredibly serious. Josh could have died."

Have you ever felt trapped, as Josh and I did at the bottom of that pit? Have you ever looked at life and said, "I don't know the way out of this"? The truth about being trapped is that you need someone outside your situation to rescue you.

THE BAD SAMARITAN

Many have told the story of the Samaritan woman before. It is usually told something like this: Jesus met a woman of ill repute at a well and asked her for water. A discussion ensued, and he revealed that he knew all about her sinful life. Feeling cornered and under conviction, the woman changed the subject and tried to argue religion with Jesus. He corrected her Samaritan worship theology, then he sent her off to fetch people from the town so he could speak to them. The whole town believed, and Jesus was a hero.

That's the story as it is often told. It's a nice story. It makes us feel good about the message of Jesus Christ. The only problem is almost everything I just said about the Samaritan woman is presumption. I suggest that the Samaritan woman is the most misunderstood woman in history.

We get her story wrong for a few reasons. First, we assume that any woman who has been married this many times is a floozy.

Second, we assume that a woman in her day and time must have *chosen* to live with a man she was not married to.

Finally, we question the rest of her actions, which seem tainted by our already low view of her. We do this because her life seems out of order from our perspective. There is an order we're supposed to do things in, right? My mother made this point to me when I headed off to college. She gave me this advice: "Son, I'm looking forward to being a mother-in-law and a grandmother—in that order."

So when we look at the Samaritan woman we see a life out of order. It doesn't fit the mold. She doesn't fit the cookie-cutter pattern many of us were cut from. When we hear of a Samaritan man who helps out a stranger, he becomes the Good Samaritan. When we hear of a Samaritan woman who is living with a guy, she becomes the Bad Samaritan. Certainly there was sin in her life, yet there are many problems with our assumptions about this supposedly bad Samaritan woman.

The first assumption, that she is a floozy, is put into question because marriage and divorce didn't work for people then the way they usually do today. Men were entirely in control of marriage and divorce in that day. Nowhere did Jesus say that she left each prior husband because she had committed adultery. It could have been that they died. Or, more likely, they divorced her. We may be meeting a woman who was not immoral but was repeatedly rejected and left for a younger woman, a common practice in that day (and not uncommon in our own). We simply don't know the reason for her circumstances.

The second assumption, that this living arrangement was her choice, doesn't take into account that she may have been kicked out by her last husband, possibly rejected in favor of another woman. It could be that he didn't give her a "certificate of divorce," a practice Jesus mentioned in Matthew 19. He reminded men, who were in control of divorce proceedings, that Moses permitted them to divorce because their "hearts were hard." A woman could not divorce a man in that culture, so she may have been legally bound to her prior husband, living with another man because it was her only way to survive.

Our third assumption is that all her actions should be questioned because of the first two assumptions. It is possible, of course, that she was responsible for part of, even most of, her circumstances. However, it is not reasonable to assume that she is at fault for everything that had happened to her. I find it odd that when we speculate about a person's life, either a biblical or a contemporary person, we typically assume the worst. We wrongly speculate that this Samaritan woman was a horrible person who finally faced a judge, albeit a benevolent one. But could it be that she was merely trapped in a cycle not entirely of her own making, and that the Savior rescued her? If we reread the story with that in mind, we see a woman with a great mind and initiative, not a villain, who, because of an encounter with Jesus, was empowered to become the hero of the story. She was not the Bad Samaritan. She was Jesus' apostle to the Samaritans.

ROCK BOTTOM

When you see someone who feels trapped in his or her circumstances, do you assume that person is at fault? Do you tend to discount the circumstances that negatively impact others but amplify your own negative circumstances to explain away your failures? It is human nature to be quick to judge the motives of others while giving ourselves a pass. In fact, it is so common, the practice has a name. It's called the "fundamental attribution error." But not all those who hit rock bottom threw themselves there.

Consider the fact that the story of the Samaritan woman comes on the heels of the story of Nicodemus the Pharisee. Nicodemus is the most opposite person we can imagine from the Samaritan woman. Yet by the end of the story, I want to be more like this woman. At the end of John 3, Nicodemus didn't yet believe; whereas at the end of chapter 4, the Samaritan woman not only believed in Jesus, but also brought others to him. Throughout their conversation Nicodemus didn't understand what the Lord was saying, but the woman repeatedly moved the conversation forward, perceptively and intelligently. She didn't get it at the start, but she was quick to recognize the truth.

THE WAY OF ESCAPE

The Samaritan woman's conversation with Jesus is the longest recorded conversation our Lord had with another person. Could it be that Jesus knew we should relate to the Samaritan woman? Jesus was a friend of sinners, so he didn't have this encounter so we might judge the woman. Perhaps Jesus knows that we, too, feel trapped sometimes, unsure how to get out of the situations we find ourselves in, whether resulting from dumb decisions, strange occurrences, or hurtful things done by others.

If we are honest with ourselves, we can admit that we often feel trapped. We feel trapped in habits we can't break. We feel trapped at work. We feel trapped in attitudes that keep rearing their ugly heads. We feel trapped in patterns of sin. We sometimes even feel trapped in our bodies, looking in the mirror and wondering, "Who is this?" Even a marriage can make you feel trapped.

It was clear that Rick was on the wrong path. He had that fake confidence people display when they know what they are doing is wrong but want to project that they are sure it is right.

Rick's marriage was in trouble, mostly because he felt trapped in it. He told me that his wife never let him do the things he wanted to, and now that he was middle-aged and their kids were out of the house, he just needed to get out. He had a plan in place: He was about to sign for an apartment and would soon move out and live the single life. He missed that life, he told me, and felt that he had grown up too fast. Being able to hang out with the guys or going hunting whenever he wanted seemed exciting to him. He was like a teenager eager to move out of his parents' house. Rick hadn't told his wife of the plan, but she knew things were bad. No adulterous acts had been committed so far, but my guess was that that would happen at the next opportunity.

As we talked, I asked Rick if he loved his wife. He absolutely did. I asked if she was at fault in all this. He didn't really think so. She had some annoying habits, but she was a pretty good woman. I asked if he thought leaving his wife would make him a better man and more like Christ. He didn't answer that one. Rick just felt trapped, and he was going to do what he could to escape that feeling. Rick couldn't see that his problem had nothing to do with his address. The solution wouldn't come in a rented bachelor pad or by separating from his wife. Deep down, I think he knew this wouldn't really work. The solution was to talk it through with his wife and grow as a husband. He needed to express his unfulfilled desires to her, not abandon her in search of a more free and spontaneous life.

It is possible that Rick's wife needed to relax a bit about what he should and shouldn't do, but she wasn't the problem. Rick was trapping himself with his own attitude.

Fortunately, Rick didn't move out and did make an effort to deepen his communication with his wife. Just a few months later, he told about going away for a hunting trip and about taking his wife on a date when he returned, and how amazing both times were. To my delight, he talked more about her than about his hunting buddies. He said their marriage was better than it had ever been.

No matter what rock and hard place makes you feel trapped, even if it is a marriage, you can escape the feeling of being trapped without running from the situation.

HAVE YOU BEEN WITH JESUS?

Jesus reaches across all kinds of barriers that trap people. Consider the barriers between Jesus and the Samaritan woman. Ethnic, economic, and educational barriers divided them. Divisions caused by geography, religion, and gender were present as well. The more we think of those divisions, the larger they loom. But there is good news: Jesus is in the barrier-breaking and bridge-building business.

The distance between God and humanity, which Jesus crossed, is so great that the distance between any two human beings is easy for him to close. The kingdom of God unites us in a higher citizenship than any of the social, racial, or ethnic identities we have constructed for ourselves.

Jesus knew the Samaritan woman felt trapped. But he's not the kind of person to either judge her and move on or merely ignore her situation to make her feel better. Jesus found a third way, higher than either judgmentalism or permissiveness. Have you been with this barrier-breaking, bridge-building Jesus?

WORSHIP WARS

I like it that the Samaritan woman didn't mince words, even after she had a sense of whom she was dealing with. She could see that he was a prophet, she said. So she got right to the point. Today, we are anything but direct. The news is rarely new. Our preaching is something closer to "speeching." Meetings tend to be about how to miss the point more intentionally, and our organizations feed the elephant in the room by never talking about it. The Samaritan woman did none of this. "If this is truly a prophet with me," she thought, "there is no sense talking about fetching water, father Jacob, or failed marriages."

One of my friends traveled overseas to a country with a culture radically different from his own. While standing in a line to greet local residents, a woman came up to him and placed both hands on the sides of his significant torso, then bounced his belly up and down. As she did that, she said in broken English, "You are so healthy!" My buddy laughed and said, "Yes I am!"

Another friend visited a country where people wanted to honor him by making a shirt for him. An elderly woman approached him with a measuring tape and proceeded to mark down his measurements. She said one word to him, then then walked away giggling. He asked the missionaries what that word meant and they told him it was a tribal word for *elephant*. The Samaritan was one of these kinds of women. She didn't avoid the "elephant" in the room. Instead, she headed straight to it.

Now for a little context. The usual reading of this story assumes that the Samaritan woman has an inadequate view of worship and that Jesus corrects it. That is not the case. Instead, this conversation came about due to the legacy of ethnic and religious violence that had plagued two people groups for centuries. "Our ancestors worshiped on this mountain, but you Jews claim that the place where we must worship is Jerusalem" (John 4:20). If ever a comment was loaded, it was this one. This statement refers to the Samaritan temple, built on a mountain in Samaria in 400 BC.[1] The Jews had reached their limit for tolerating the worship practices of their "half-breed" Samaritan cousins. So they marched up to Samaria and tore down the temple of worship. People died. Sacred places were defiled. It was like a church bombing, mosque burning, or synagogue shooting in its day, but worse. It wasn't the act of a solitary terrorist; it was a state-sanctioned religious attack to destroy the way of life of a minority ethnic group that worshiped the same God but in a different way.

This is the key to understanding the tension that existed between the Samaritans and the Jews. So we cannot think of this as an isolated conversation between two people who were somewhat different from one another. No, this was like a conversation between an IRA soldier and a British priest, or a Palestinian refugee talking with an influential rabbi. Do you think you have a "worship war" in your congregation? Jews and Samaritans took it to a whole new level.

The difference in this encounter is that the rabbi in John 4 was the Son of God. So he didn't get caught up in the worship wars of the moment; instead, he pointed the Samaritan woman to worship in the way of the kingdom. He knew that *whom* we worship matters more than *how* we worship. Whatever the "right" way to worship is, Jesus certainly knows it better than any of us. So he gave it to her: "Woman . . . believe me, a time is coming when you will worship the Father neither on this mountain nor in Jerusalem. You Samaritans worship what you do not know; we worship what we do know, for salvation is from the Jews. Yet a time is coming and has now come when the true worshipers will worship the Father in the Spirit and in truth, for they are the kind of worshipers the Father seeks. God is spirit, and his worshipers must worship in the Spirit and in truth" (vv. 21–24).

Believe me . . .

Perhaps this is more than just a saying. Worship starts with believing in him.

Neither on this mountain nor in Jerusalem . . .

This was a radical thing for a rabbi to say. To diminish Jerusalem would have been a non-starter for Jews on the subject of worship. If the woman wasn't hooked yet, she was at that point. This was new information. Jesus didn't gloss over that there were problems with the way the Samaritans worship. He noted that they *worship what they do not know.* However, that point is moot because a new way of worship supersedes both systems.

Salvation is from the Jews . . .

The woman may have heard this as just another assertion that the Jewish way was better than the Samaritan way—though she found out just a few seconds later that this rabbi was salvation itself. The word he used, *soteria* in the original language, means "deliverance," "preservation," "safety," or "messianic salvation." These have become Christian code words for Jesus, of course. It's as if he were saying, "Well, salvation *is* from the Jews—I am salvation in the flesh, and I am a Jew."

True worshipers . . .

The kind of worshipers God seeks are true worshipers. I think we all want to be true worshipers. It is great to know that you don't have to go seeking God. If you worship in this way, he'll find you. There are no crowds of seekers in worship. There is only one True Seeker in a crowd of true worshipers. But how do these true worshipers worship?

In the Spirit and in truth . . .

In two words Jesus defined the aims and the means of worship. It begins with the spirit of the worshiper: the motives, the heart, and the desires. If our focus is upon God, we have aimed at the only true goal in worship. So a focus on the self, on our appearance, on our reputation— these are distractions. True worshipers are undistracted by self. And they focus on God in truth. This sets true worship apart from a more abstract form of meditation. In true worship, we do not merely remove self from our focus; we put into focus the eternal truth of Jesus Christ. True worship is not mere emptying but emptying as a prelude to a filling. When our worship is focusing upon God's truth, we become filled with the Spirit of God, overflowing. We are poured out so we might be filled up again, in him.

MESSIAH

The Samaritan woman was having not only the longest recorded conversation with the Son of God, but also one of the most theologically meaty conversations on the subject of worship. But she was not done yet. She acknowledged that this Jewish rabbi spoke some sense. But she was not ready to buy it all. She was holding back the one card she still had to play in this conversation: the Messiah card.

Samaritans were eager to see the Messiah come. For this geopolitically marginalized people, poor and outcast, rejected and oppressed even by the Jews—who were likewise rejected and oppressed by the Romans, the bigger fish in the bigger pond—the idea of a coming king who would restore order to the world was undeniably attractive. The Samaritan woman picked up on the messianic overtones of the way Jesus spoke. He said things like "a time is coming" (v. 21) and later noted that it "has now come" (v. 23), and she rightly read "Messiah" between the lines of this sermonette on worship.

"The woman said, 'I know that Messiah' (called Christ) 'is coming. When he comes, he will explain everything to us'" (v. 25).

When we're trapped, it's easy to believe that "a time is coming" when things will be different but not realize that it "has now come." The woman missed it. She played her final card with the rabbi, her Messiah card, and when she turned it over she couldn't help noticing that the face on the card resembled the man before her. When she said that the Christ will explain things, Jesus said, in effect, "That's my last name." She talked as if she knew what was what, but Jesus told her who was who.

Like many of us who feel trapped, the Samaritan woman believed a time was coming—salvation would come sometime in the future. Her life was in shambles. She couldn't escape it. She was violating her own conscience by living with a man, perhaps having no other options. A "someday Savior" was her only thread of hope. The words of her statement may sound like hope, but between the lines there is a sound of despair. We strike that same note with our "someday Savior" statements.

"My marriage is on the rocks and I'm having an affair, but someday I'll look back and see it worked together for good."

"Your son has leukemia, but someday you'll see him in heaven again and it will be all right. Every tear will be wiped from your eyes."

"I have debt up to my eyeballs and can't stop spending, but someday my ship will come in and I'll be fine."

This thinking is hollow. These statements are hopeful words wrapped around hopeless situations, greeting-card theology pasted atop life's deepest problems. Remember the truth about being trapped: You need someone outside your situation to rescue you.

Jesus is the Christ who *has* come, not one that merely is coming. Jesus corrects our hopeless thinking just as he did the Samaritan woman's. Jesus is not only a future hope for salvation—he is a present-reality Savior who can change everything, starting with freeing you from whatever you are trapped in, regardless of how you got there.

THE BUMBLING DISCIPLES

Jesus has played things perfectly leading to this crescendo of the conversation. If this were a baseball game, it would be the bottom of the ninth, bases loaded, count full. All that would be left would be the winning homerun. If it were an election, it would be locked in an Electoral College stalemate with everything coming down to one swing vote. In some church traditions, the organist would be vibrating high-pitched tones, ladies' hankies would be waving, and old men would be offering deep-throated "Amens." All that would be left is the altar call.

But there is no grand slam, no dramatic vote count, no running down the aisles. Instead, the disciples returned from grocery shopping. Peter and Andrew had bagel crumbs on their beards. Thomas sloshed a jug of the local brew, while Judas collared Bartholomew for reneging on the check. Meanwhile, James and John bickered over who would get the last falafel.

As they returned, Jesus seems to have been thinking, "You chuckle-heads always have the worst timing." The Samaritan woman didn't say another word; she slipped away and the conversation was over.

It is as if the batter struck out, the voters demanded a recount, and the organist hit a sour note. The banter of the disciples cuts short this beautiful conversation by asking if Jesus wanted some grub.

Jesus replied, "I have food to eat that you know nothing about" (v. 32).

Jesus' disciples tended to take his words literally when he meant figuratively, and vice versa. This was one of those cases. The food that has fed Jesus' soul is not baked bread, any more than the living water he offered the Samaritan woman was drawn from a well. The difference was that the Samaritan woman figured out Jesus' meaning through questioning. The disciples didn't. Jesus was sustained by something more than calories. He explained, "My food . . . is to do the will of him who sent me and to finish his work" (v. 34).

Even this seems to have a double meaning. First, he must finish the work he's begun with the Samaritan woman. The hook was set, and he planned to reel in her whole community.

Second, he must finish the entire work, work that ends with a bloody cross and an empty tomb. This activity in Samaria is part of "the time that has now come." Jesus and his disciples were headed north to Galilee, through Samaria, but this was merely a brief detour before descending south again. Jesus would descend even to hell if he must in order to bring salvation from the Jews to people like the Samaritan woman and her fellow villagers.

The Samaritan woman left her jar at the well just as the disciples had earlier left their nets at the boat. She had found Living Water after all, and no longer needed a jar. Her thirst was quenched not by the well Jacob dug but with Jesus' vision of true worship. Meanwhile, the disciples tried to figure out what Jesus meant about bread and harvest. (Jesus noted the contrast between her as a hero of the story and the poor-timing disciples in verses 35–38, explaining that because other people have done the hard labor, the disciples will reap the benefit.) What the Samaritan woman did next produced immediate results.

No longer trapped in this cycle of shame, the woman felt free to share her faith with her town. She was trapped at the bottom of a dry well but then was lifted up by Christ. She now overflowed with living water as he had elevated her to be his evangelist. The Samaritan woman became the first person in all of Scripture to lead her non-Jewish neighbors to the truth of Jesus Christ. Before Paul was the apostle to the Gentiles, this woman became an apostle to the Samaritans.

"Many of the Samaritans from that town believed in him because of the woman's testimony," says verse 39. Nothing empowers like freedom. The woman no longer cared what people thought of her, and she went from avoiding the crowd because of her reputation to seeking out the crowd. This rabbi at the well, who knew all about her deepest heartaches and failures, cast a vision for her of a new day, one that had now come. What Jesus knew about her didn't taint his love for her. This is how Jesus works. He knows everything about you and still loves you.

Whether through a trusted friend or by miraculous provision, escape from a trap depends on help from the outside. You may feel like you are at the bottom of a pit, barely able to breathe because of the stress of your situation. If so, know that Jesus is the escape. You may be looking to other sources: success, mentors, jobs, money, learning, approval, parents. But only Jesus has the living water. Become a true worshiper of the true Messiah, for he is your source of escape.

Many people you know may feel trapped as well. Don't assume that they threw themselves to the rock-bottom position they are in. Have compassion. And drink Jesus' living water so you can offer living water to them.

PRAYER

You are with me, Jesus. Even though I feel like I'm not entirely responsible for the situations I'm in, I do admit that I haven't done all I could have to prevent them. You know everything I've ever done and still love me, but I feel trapped at times and need your help from the outside. Help me. And help me to help others out of their confining circumstances—and to keep from judging. Thank you, Jesus, my rescuer!

FOR REFLECTION

1. How might others misinterpret or misread your circumstances? Do you think Jesus sees you differently than others do? What might he say to you about other people?

2. Read John 4:1–42. Does an adjusted perspective of the Samaritan woman give you specific encouragement about your circumstances? What does Jesus say to her that you need to hear as well?

3. Have you ever tried to change the subject with Jesus? What are some hot topics today you like to talk about that distract from what Jesus wants to say to you?

4. In what ways do you feel trapped? In what ways do you need the transforming presence of Jesus to set you free?

4
POWERLESS

JOHN 4:43–54

The Harry Potter series by J. K. Rowling was rejected by publishers twelve times before getting into print. Stephen King's first novel was rejected more than twice that number. Albert Einstein failed his college entrance exam, and Vincent van Gogh sold only one painting in his lifetime. Harrison Ford was told he didn't have what it took to be a star, and Michael Jordan was cut from his high school basketball team. Even Walt Disney was fired from one job because he lacked imagination and had no good ideas. Rejection often precedes success.

Bill Gates's first company failed. (It was called Traf-O-Data, so no wonder.) Ben Franklin had only a few years of formal schooling. Jerry Seinfeld got booed off the stage the first time he did standup. Jim Carrey was once homeless. Winston Churchill flunked the sixth grade. Ludwig van Beethoven went deaf. Oprah Winfrey was sexually abused and became pregnant at the age of fourteen. Those who succeed in life often must overcome major barriers.

We love hearing stories like these because they inspire us to overcome. They help us see the success light at the end of our seemingly endless tunnel of failure and shortcomings. Nothing succeeds like failure, we are told. And that is true. But there is a flip side to that coin.

Nothing fails like success.

HAVE YOU BEEN WITH JESUS?

When all is going well and you think you have everything you need in life, that is often the moment when the world comes crashing in. Past success is no protection from future failure. Have you experienced that before? Just when everything started to click . . . it happened. Your work, family, social, and even spiritual life may all go swimmingly, then you hear the news.

Medical test results arrive. *Positive.*

Written notice received. *Termination.*

Final papers served. *Divorce.*

Crying teenager confesses. *Pregnancy.*

Governing board announces. *Layoff.*

Trusted colleague resigns. *Embezzlement.*

Dreaded phone rings. *Death.*

Have your mountaintops ever been followed by deep, dark valleys? No matter how successful you are, it can all come tumbling down in one moment. In fact, the pain of tragedy is often accentuated by how well things were going up until the crisis. Everything seemed too good to be true . . . and it was.

TOO GOOD TO BE TRUE

The royal official of John 4 had it good before he had it bad. He was a big shot. To the bystander, a royal official in the service of the ruler of Israel would have had everything going for him. He had the right connections and the right education. He had the power to make decisions that would impact hundreds, if not thousands, of lives. And where he didn't have political power, he had money. Financial means are another source of power, one that seems to influence everyone. He could buy what he wanted and, in a tight spot, bribe his way out of trouble.

A royal official would have had the symbols of success too. He would have had the mansion in the right part of town, the summer home on the Sea of Galilee, the *GQ*-worthy robes, and the silver Mercedes-Benz chariot.

He had the right stuff. He was an overwhelming success. He was in charge. But he wasn't in control.[1] This became clear when his son got sick.

"There was a certain royal official whose son lay sick at Capernaum" (John 4:46).

At first it seemed simple. Just a little bug. A cough here and there. A few days in bed. Then it got worse. Home remedies didn't work. Fluids went right through him. No food stayed down.

The doctors were brought in. The best care money could buy; still no progress. After the doctors came the priests. Sacrifices, candles, and prayers were offered, but to no avail. Neither medicine nor meditation did the trick. His son was dying.

What would the royal official have traded to see his son well? Money? Surely. Position, power, and possessions? Absolutely. As he looked upon his son writhing in agony, he would have given up the mansion, the summer home, and the chariot just for one pain-free night with his boy. But he couldn't. A man who could command people, give orders, hire and fire employees, a man who was in charge—that man found that he wasn't in control.

Have you discovered this? What experience proved the point to you? Not to worry, being out of control is the best place to be, for only then can you let Jesus take control. The presence of Jesus changes everything for those powerless to change anything.

TRUST AND CONTROL

When speaking at a retreat for church leaders in Kansas, I talked about trust. I told them I could measure their level of trust with one another through a simple exercise: I handed my cell phone to the person on my left and asked each person to do the same. They did. I said, "I can tell how trusting you are by how quickly you take your phone back from that person." Everyone laughed, somewhat nervously.

Then I just moved on to my next point. One by one they started to reach over and snatch their phones back. Within five seconds, half of them had their phones in their own hands. Within ten seconds, everyone had grabbed their phones, and many were already checking for missed messages.

I paused and told them they had only confirmed what is true for most all of us: Due to our addiction to technology, we tend to have about ten seconds of trust in us. We all agreed we had a lot of work to do.

We have a hard time trusting others because we like control, especially over something like a cell phone. We want to control every portion of our lives that we can. But we sometimes have to admit that no matter what we are in charge of, we are not entirely in control.

This man in John 4 is called "a certain royal official" (v. 46). In the English language this just means "a *specific* royal official." But when I read the word *certain*, I can't help but think about how *certain* the royal official was before his son became sick. He was certain of so much—certain of himself, his power, and his education. He was certain he could provide for his family and protect them from harm. He was certain that he was the most successful of all his friends and the bright shining hope of his extended family. He was certain people were jealous of him and that his investments would only go up and to the right.

But it just took one sick kid to make this certain royal official not so certain anymore. Uncertainty creeps into a certain life, no matter who you are. "For He makes His sun rise on the evil and on the good, and sends rain on the just and on the unjust" (Matt. 5:45 NKJV).

ALL BECOME BEGGARS

When the royal official "heard that Jesus had arrived in Galilee from Judea, he went to him and begged him to come and heal his son, who was close to death" (John 4:47). At the end of his rope, the royal official heard of a man who was doing miracles. He tossed rationality out the door and chased hope in the form of a miracle-worker he'd never seen. He cared not for his position or authority or the whispers this would cause in circles of power. Instead, he asked Jesus for help, even begged for it. This was a big deal for anyone in that culture, where pride was prized above all else.

The word used and the way it's used in the original language reveals that this man was begging Jesus repeatedly for help.[2] He just wouldn't stop. The royal official stood in a long line of successful people who ended up begging for mercy when their children were at risk.

The great King David of Israel had a kingdom at his command, but when his baby became ill to the point of death, "David begged God to spare the child. He went without food and lay all night on the bare ground" (2 Sam. 12:16 NLT).

Another of the powerful religious elite, Jairus, a ruler of a synagogue, fell at the feet of Jesus to plead his case "and begged Him earnestly, saying, 'My little daughter lies at the point of death. Come and lay Your hands on her, that she may be healed, and she will live'" (Mark 5:22–23 NKJV). When a woman from Tyre, who was in a similar situation with her little girl, heard Jesus was in town, she "came and fell at his feet. Her little girl was possessed by an evil spirit, and she begged him to cast out the demon from her daughter" (Mark 7:25–26 NLT).

Sometimes there is nothing left to do but beg when our own health is at risk: "While Jesus was in one of the towns, a man came along who was covered with leprosy. When he saw Jesus, he fell with his face to the ground and begged him, 'Lord, if you are willing, you can make me clean'" (Luke 5:12).

Even Paul himself, writer of nearly half the New Testament and apostle to the Gentiles, pleaded for God's healing of a major physical infirmity: "To keep me from becoming proud, I was given a thorn in my flesh, a messenger from Satan to torment me and keep me from becoming proud. Three different times I begged the Lord to take it away" (2 Cor. 12:7–8 NLT).

Sometimes world events leave us helpless and vulnerable. Esther was the powerful queen to the Persian emperor, but when her people were threatened with genocide, even she "went again before the king, falling down at his feet and begging him with tears to stop the evil plot . . . against the Jews" (Est. 8:3 NLT). She did so even though she had to risk her own death for entering his court without being invited.

Sometimes the economy is what gets us, or at least the part of the economy that doesn't seem to work for us. The servant mentioned in Matthew 18 had accumulated a fortune of debt and lived off the profits of his ventures, but when his plans failed, "he couldn't pay, so his master ordered that he be sold—along with his wife, his children, and everything he owned—to pay the debt. But the man fell down before his master and begged him, 'Please, be patient with me, and I will pay it all'" (Matt. 18:25–26 NLT).

Each of these people, whose lives had once seemed firmly under their control, ended up begging. All become beggars eventually. You may be a king or a queen, a lawyer or a doctor, a mom or a dad, a pastor or a hairstylist—no matter who you are, the time of begging comes. When the going got tough and Jesus showed up, even the "demons begged, 'If you cast us out, send us into that herd of pigs'" (Matt. 8:31 NLT).

Everywhere Jesus turns, people in need beg for him. Why? Jesus is powerful. Begging of Jesus is the last resort for those who believe they are in control but the first resort of the wise. Have you experienced this? When you see these powerful people on Beggars Lane, would you hold up a "Me Too" sign? If so, don't worry. There is hope. If you beg of the One with the power to answer your prayers, you will find more than hope. You will find the help that is not available elsewhere.

EXPECTING YOUR GOLDEN TICKET

"They begged him to let the sick touch at least the fringe of his robe, and all who touched him were healed" (Matt. 14:36 NLT). I love this line: "All who touched him were healed." All. Yes, *all*.

Touching Jesus' jeans is a better means of grace than anything in your world. (Yes, I picture Jesus wearing jeans, at least on the weekends. Sorry if you're more into the robe-and-sandals Jesus.) If Jesus drops lint out of a pocket, there is more divine power in that lint than in any institution, government, or ministry you might reach out to for help. A napkin Jesus used would break eBay's servers because it would be such a popular item. In a crisis, we grasp for all kinds of solutions. But begging of Jesus is the best place to start, especially when you think you're in charge but find you are not in control.

After a bit of begging, "the royal official said, 'Sir, come down before my child dies.' 'Go,' Jesus replied, 'your son will live.' The man took Jesus at his word and departed" (John 4:49–50).

That last part is tricky for us of little faith. The man in crisis, the man who begged, then took Jesus at his word. Do you? Are you willing to not only beg, but also believe? That is what Jesus looks for:

those who are both humble enough to admit that they've lost control of the situation and trusting enough to take Jesus at his word.

The royal official headed home, and "while he was still on the way, his servants met him with the news that his boy was living" (v. 51). Only while he was on the way, after the act of faith, did he get the news.

This is how it works, doesn't it? We trust Jesus; we go on our way. And while we are "on the way" of life, his miracles come as promised.

My family's favorite movie is *Willy Wonka and the Chocolate Factory.* The movie centers on an impoverished little boy who wants to win a golden ticket to tour the chocolate factory. He is depressed because he hasn't gotten one, though he's bought just two of the many candy bars where only five tickets are stashed. Finally, there is only one golden ticket left to be redeemed among thousands and thousands of candy bars for sale. The boy visits his mother, who is working late doing laundry for others. His mother tries to cheer him up, saying, "Charlie, you'll get your chance. One day things will change."

"When?" the melancholy boy says. "When will they change?"

"Probably when you least expect it."[3]

It takes great faith to beg for a miracle in your crisis. It takes even greater faith to expect it and stop searching anxiously for it. For the powerless one, the one out of control, Jesus' provision shows up when you least expect it, after you've stopped begging for it. This is true faith.

The royal official wanted to confirm his hunch, so "when he inquired as to the time when his son got better, they said to him, 'Yesterday, at one in the afternoon, the fever left him.' Then the father realized that this was the exact time at which Jesus had said to him, 'Your son will live.' So he and his whole household believed" (vv. 52–53).

THE NICU

Until my first child was born, I didn't have any idea what a NICU was. It's a hospital acronym. And stands for one of the scariest phrases a new parent can hear.

Everything was going well in our lives. I had a new job lined up. We had a new house to move into. Our old house had sold quickly. To top it off, we got the good the news: pregnant! We had been hoping, and now we were excited.

Everything seemed just right. The pregnancy: uncomfortable but eventless. The heartbeat: fast but steady. The labor: long but normal. After a final push, he screamed into the world. A boy! Maxim Keith Philip Drury was born on June 17, 2000, and this millennium baby, born on the most even of years, had an even number of fingers and toes, eyes and ears. Everything seemed right, even perfect.

Except the doctor didn't hand the boy over to Mommy right away. They placed him on a special table. After a few orders were given that I didn't understand, a nurse left, then returned with a half dozen other medical personnel I'd never seen.

"What's wrong?" we asked.

"We don't yet know," a nurse said. "His heartbeat skyrocketed, and his color is off." They rushed our baby out of the room. "Where are you going?" we asked.

"To the NICU."

"What's that?"

"Neonatal Intensive Care Unit."

After I'd spent a few minutes making sure my wife was OK, she sent me off to the NICU to watch over the son that neither of us had yet held. As I walked from Kathy's room, completely uncertain about what was happening to our only child, I was overcome by the most intense emotions I had felt in my life.

I cried and prayed my way down the hallway, and found my son in an incubator, with more wires and tubes attached to him than I could count.

"Please," I begged. "Please, please, please."

Sometimes "Please!" is the only prayer we know how to pray. Yet God knows the request. Even when "we do not know what we ought to pray for . . . the Spirit himself intercedes for us through wordless groans" (Rom. 8:26). I would have traded the new job in an instant for the answer to that prayer. I would have given away the old house and the new one. I would have offered my very life. I begged. I had thought I was in charge of my life, but everything that mattered was out of my control. I couldn't even hold my son to comfort him. I was powerless. I only knew that the presence of Jesus changes everything for those powerless to change anything.

God answered that one-word, beggar's prayer. Max made it. A few days later, we got to take him home.

Jesus has the power to answer the most desperate prayers. When you find yourself there with the royal official, as I did, pray to Jesus. Beg, if you must. He has the power to meet the challenge. In a remarkably similar story recorded in Matthew 8:5–13, a centurion whose servant was sick asked Jesus to heal him. Jesus was willing to go to the centurion's house, but he replied, "Lord, I do not deserve to have you come under my roof. But just say the word, and my servant will be healed. For I myself am a man under authority, with soldiers under me. I tell this one, 'Go,' and he goes; and that one, 'Come,' and he comes. I say to my servant, 'Do this,' and he does it'" (8:8–9). Jesus spoke the servant's healing, and he was healed that very hour.

We forget the power of Jesus. Perhaps for too long we've pictured him as we see him in the popular paintings, having blonde hair, blue eyes, soft skin, and holding a baby lamb in his arms. Remember that Jesus is the commander of the army of the Lord (Josh. 5:13–14). When the soldiers came to get Jesus in the garden, asking for Jesus of Nazareth, he said the words "I am he," and the soldiers "drew back and fell to the ground" (John 18:5–6).

Later, Jesus stood before the Roman governor, Pilate, the most powerful man in that region, and Jesus threw Pilate's power back in his face, saying, "You would have no power over me if it were not given to you from above" (19:11).

When Peter responded to Jesus' arrest by pulling a sword and slashing a servant of the high priest, Jesus stopped him, saying, "Do you think I cannot call on my Father, and he will at once put at my disposal more than twelve legions of angels?" (Matt. 26:53). That would be some seventy thousand angels! Jesus is basically the top general of the greatest army in the universe.

Significantly, Jesus said this just a short time after he himself had passionately begged, "My Father, if it is possible, may this cup be taken from me" (v. 39). Jesus knew full well what it means to be struggling in life's circumstances. Yet the Supreme Power of the universe nevertheless accepted the cup that is the consequence of human separation from God. He didn't assert control, but instead submitted to his Father: "Yet not as I will, but as you will" (v. 39). Even when the Son of God was afraid and knew what awaited him, he nevertheless went to the One who could help him and did the only thing any human can and should: He beseeched God. And the Father was with him. He did not get the specific answer he requested, but he begged just like you and I might.

Right now, remember your time of desperation, the last time you begged God to deliver you, to answer, to be present. Now think of what you need today. What makes you feel powerless? What thing reminds you that you are in charge but not in control? What do you feel the need to beg God for today?

Whatever you're begging him for, know that he has the power to do it. Regardless of the prospects or outcome, ask him now. The presence of Jesus changes everything for those powerless to change anything.

PRAYER

You are with me, Jesus. I am so glad that is true—because I so badly need you. I am facing something I am powerless to overcome. I know I can't control everything. I ask you, beg you, to show up in this situation, because I need your power. Thank you, Jesus, my God!

FOR REFLECTION

1. Think of a situation in which you felt powerless. How bad did it get? Did you come to the point of begging? If not, do you know someone who did?

2. Read Joshua 5:13–14; John 18:4–6; 19:11; and Matthew 26:53. How do these verses depicting the power of Jesus Christ give you strength?

3. Have you ever seen God at work in an unmistakable way? What was it like before God moved, and how did things change after he was clearly present?

4. What major problem in your life can you trust God with today? What will it feel like to admit you are not in control of that situation? Are there parts of it that will feel hard? Are there other parts that will feel freeing?

5
STUCK

JOHN 5:1–15

Distress calls came out of the South Pacific on Christmas Eve 2013. A ship had ventured 2,250 miles south of Tasmania into the icy waters surrounding Antarctica. This was intentional; more than fifty scientists aboard the Russian vessel *Akademik Shokalskiy* were there to study the increase in ice calving off glaciers, thus shrinking the glaciers themselves and increasing ice floes in the frigid waters surrounding our coldest continent.

The *Akademik Shokalskiy* (don't worry, I can't pronounce it either) got stuck in the very ice the scientists were studying. So the rescue calls went out. The Chinese icebreaker *Xue Long* (meaning "Snow Dragon") responded to the stranded ship. Icebreakers have reinforced hulls and a shape designed to push through sea ice. However, even the powerful *Xue Long* became icebound. The rescuers now needed rescuing. The *Xue Long* dispatched its helicopter to evacuate the scientists on the Russian vessel, ferrying them to the Australian vessel *Aurora Australis*, which remained in open water. Finally, the US Coast Guard icebreaker *Polar Star* was dispatched to free the multiple ships stuck in Antarctic waters. The winds shifted, however, and the ice moved away from the *Akademik Shokalskiy* and *Xue Long*, and both ships were able to sail out under their own power and the international ordeal involving four ships from four countries was over.[1]

Being stuck in ice near the South Pole sounds like a horrible way to spend the holidays. Imagine being stuck in a helpless situation for thirty-eight years. That was the condition of a man described in chapter 5 of the gospel of John. For thirty-eight years he had been completely stuck because of his inability to walk. He was utterly dependent on other people. He couldn't do what most everyone takes for granted. He couldn't get himself out of bed. He couldn't get himself to the restroom. He couldn't enjoy family life. He was completely, physically stuck.

The biblical word used to describe the man means "weakness of the body" or "infirmity." We don't know precisely what condition the man had; we only know that he couldn't get up and walk, and that he had been in this state for thirty-eight years.

There was little to alleviate this disabled man's suffering in his day. They didn't have wheelchairs, and medical treatments were few. The disabled people of Jerusalem had three options: They could stay at home alone; they could prevail upon a friend or family member to deposit them in a high traffic area so they could beg for money; or they could go to the Pool of Bethesda, where people occasionally received miraculous healing. This disabled man seemed to have chosen the third option over and over again. For years, perhaps decades, he was brought to this same location, seeking healing. He chose not to lie alone at home nor subject himself to the humiliation of begging. Instead, he spent his time seeking the long shot, the lucky roll, the random miracle rumored to be possible at the Pool of Bethesda.

John gives some context for this place where the disabled man spent his days: "There is in Jerusalem near the Sheep Gate a pool, which in Aramaic is called Bethesda and which is surrounded by five covered colonnades. Here a great number of disabled people used to lie—the blind, the lame, the paralyzed" (vv. 5:2–3).

My grandmother on my father's side spent a long time in a similar place. I bet you've visited one yourself: a nursing home. I don't like nursing homes; most of us don't, nor do most of the people who live in them. But they adjust. My grandmother did. Eventually.

I remember that during our family visits to the nursing home, my grandmother would refer to the staff as "all these German ladies that work here." This confused us because most of the employees were African-American. The riddle was solved when we remembered that she grew up in the state of Pennsylvania where the "Pennsylvania Dutch" housewives of her youth were of a more, shall we say, rotund sort. We noticed that many of the women working in the nursing home were also a bit stout. So in her mind, the women caring for her were "Germans," regardless of their true ethnicity. We weren't sure whether to be encouraged by the absence of racial prejudice in her or horrified by the deeper prejudices that may merely have concealed it.

In earlier life, as a middle-aged woman, my grandmother kept the dining room table decked out in her finest china at all times; she wanted any important guest who arrived unannounced to find her a ready host. In an apartment attached to our home, where she took up residence after my grandfather died, she kept the kitchen table set with four beautiful table settings for years. Later she moved into an intermediate care apartment, and set her tiny kitchenette with two full place settings of fine china. By the time she moved into a nursing home, all her china and silver had been placed in storage or passed on to others. But she took a full set of plastic tableware in the nursing home with her. In her room she kept an entire setting of plastic utensils, plate, and cup on her nightstand. This symbolic gesture told her true feeling: "I might be in this place that feels disgraceful to me, but I'm still me."

I think of my grandmother's shrinking world and how she clung to that shred of her dignity whenever I think of the Pool of Bethesda. At the pool were scores, perhaps hundreds, of people, desperate for healing and trying to maintain the dignity of personhood. I wonder how the place smelled. I wonder if there were sounds of wailing in pain. I wonder if some had lost their minds. If so, it would have been like many nursing homes. And the sufferers at Bethesda didn't have the benefit of hard-working, heavy-lifting "German women" to attend them as my grandmother did. They were there alone in their pain.

They came to Bethesda, hobbling, or were dropped off by busy relatives. They might be visited from time to time, but less often with each passing year. Why did they come to Bethesda? Apparently it was renowned as a place of healing long before, and for some time after, this episode in John 5.

Bethesda, in the original language, can have a double meaning. On the one hand, it can mean "shame" or "disgrace." This makes sense in the original context. The people who gathered in this location at that time in history must have felt a great sense of shame for their condition because such ailments were frequently attributed to some sin in the life of the sick person. The disciples held this mistaken thinking until Jesus corrected them in John 9:2–3.

On the other hand, Bethesda can mean "house of mercy" or "house of grace." This double meaning was likely intentional. Bethesda was a place where those who felt shame could seek mercy, a place where those who, in their culture, were disgraced by their dependence on others could receive healing grace.

It was to this place on the map where people with shame and disgrace lay, those who were seeking mercy and grace; and it is in this very place that Jesus showed up. This changed everything, of course. Those seeking grace never need to look further when he who invented it arrives, the One who embodies the concept of grace. The presence of Jesus brings miracle-moving grace to those who are stuck.

HAVE YOU BEEN WITH JESUS?

Perhaps you too struggle with a physical infirmity. If so, you can probably relate to the disabled man at the Pool of Bethesda. Perhaps you have been waiting, if not thirty-eight years then perhaps as many months or days. Maybe this ailment is something you've lived with your whole life. Like you, the disabled man waited for a miracle that never seemed to come or was missed by the slightest of margins.

It could be that you have the other kind of infirmity Bethesda represents. More often than not the word *infirmity* or *sickness* is translated in the New Testament as "weakness." Sometimes it is a physical weakness, but often it is a spiritual one. Perhaps you have been stuck in some spiritual weakness, an infirmity of the soul, and you cannot escape. Unlike a physically disabled person, whose struggles are more apparent, you may have an unseen disability. You are weak in the face of temptation. You are weakened by lust, weakened by envy, or weakened by pride. You find yourself weak from the years of fruitless struggle. You are weak from the heartache of a loved one lost in this life, or a loved one spiritually lost from God.

When you imagine this story, do you think of yourself among the disciples of Jesus, looking down at the disabled man lying on his mat, stuck in his situation? No, you're not them.

You are the disabled one.

You look up to Jesus, trying to tell your story. Expressing to him that you've been in this situation for what seems like forever. It doesn't feel fair. It's not right. Others don't have to face this. Yes, others might be worse off, but you would have so much more potential if you didn't have to deal with this disability in your body or your soul. And so you confess to him, Jesus, that you too are stuck. You are like the icebreakers *Akademik Shokalskiy* and *Xue Long*, trapped in your surroundings. You are stuck right there along with the others at the Pool of Bethesda.

Regardless of whether you are stuck physically or spiritually, Jesus shows up at your own Pool of Bethesda and asks a question. It is the same question he asked the disabled man in John 5: "When Jesus saw him lying there and learned that he had been in this condition for a long time, he asked him, 'Do you want to get well?'" (v. 6).

This seems like the most inappropriate question Jesus could have asked. Isn't this a *cruel* question? He might as well have said, "How's the view from down there, buddy?" Was Jesus really asking this man if he'd rather keep his disability? Are we missing something?

Jesus' question clarified things for the disabled man and all of us suffering from physical or spiritual weakness. To that question, anyone might respond, "Of course I want to get well." Yet Jesus stands there, in front of the literal or figurative disabled ones, including you and me, and he embodies our best chance for healing. Of course we want to get well. Yet we do not pursue the One who might make us well, any more than the disabled man at Bethesda did.

My friend Sia M'Bayo came to Christ in dramatic fashion (more on that in chapter 6), but she didn't have a church home. She visited several churches to tell them about the community center she worked at, and at every one she found apathy and disinterest. Then she visited our church. She went to a Sunday school class to inform people about the community center and their need for food, funds, and volunteers, then stayed for the rest of the class and visited the worship service.

I would never have sent Sia to the particular class she chose. That reveals some biases in me, perhaps, but the class she went to was not one I would have considered the best introduction to our church. It was a group of some sixty-five or more retirees, most of whom had lived sixty-five or more years. The class had been together for a long, long time. In fact, somewhere in the distant past, this group had been known as the young adult class. By now, the current young adults referred to it as "the old people's class." They were a room full of old, white, churchy people; not the first place I would have sent a young, African-American, single mother who had been dealing drugs just a few years before.

To my delight, the people in that class came through big time. They welcomed Sia, listened as she told about her ministry, and soon began to support it and volunteer. She attended the class for several weeks and was impressed with the passion and real-life testimonies of the people. They were living out their faith in their later years in a way that spoke volumes to her. She had finally found a group of people who weren't merely seeking healing from sin but had been healed from sin. She found Christians who wanted to get well rather than just complain about their spiritual ailments.

The disabled man at the Pool of Bethesda had been going through the motions for so long that he missed the fact that Jesus' question pointed directly at him.

"'Sir,' the invalid replied, 'I have no one to help me into the pool when the water is stirred. While I am trying to get in, someone else goes down ahead of me'" (v. 7).

The disabled man had a system he thought would get him well. He had it all figured out. When the water was stirred someday, he was going to get his shot—he'd get in the water and be the miracle story that year. But his system wasn't working for him yet. Whenever the stirring happened, he didn't have enough help to be the first one in. Someone else always beat him and was blessed ahead of him. This makes me wonder if there was some ranking system for who got to be closest to the water. Were there people there who had been there longer than thirty-eight years? Was there a seniority system? A lottery? Or was it just a disabled dog-eat-dog world at the Pool of Bethesda?

Jesus asked the man him if he wanted to get well, not why he wasn't well. But the man answered the second question, missing the point that it was Jesus, right there in front of him, who could heal him. Jesus was the one who could get him unstuck. Jesus specializes in helping the physically and spiritually stuck get unstuck. By focusing on the system he hoped would get him unstuck, the disabled man missed the One who could heal him with just a word.

Despite this, Jesus offered mercy to the one feeling shame. He gave grace to the disgraced: "Then Jesus said to him, 'Get up! Pick up your mat and walk.' At once the man was cured; he picked up his mat and walked" (vv. 8–9).

Jesus heals.

He has the power to do what all our systems hope to achieve. And he can do it "at once."

The man was healed, but the drama was just beginning, because "the day on which this took place was a Sabbath, and so the Jewish leaders said to the man who had been healed, 'It is the Sabbath; the law forbids you to carry your mat'" (vv. 9–10).

So here we are, back to the Sabbath law. Jesus did a no-no, having compassion on someone on the Sabbath. The Jewish leaders missed the point. They continued to do so even after the man clarified that this "violation" came about as a result of a healing. The disabled man replied, "The man who made me well said to me, 'Pick up your mat and walk.'" So the Jewish leaders asked, "'Who is this fellow who told you to pick it up and walk?' The man who was healed had no idea who it was, for Jesus had slipped away into the crowd that was there" (vv. 11–13).

PHARISEE 2.0

I visited a new church that a friend of mine had started in the Washington, DC, area. All kinds of young people were showing up to this ministry and finding God. It was great to see. However, they broke all the traditional rules for what "doing church" is supposed to look like. The congregation was mostly people new to the faith, so when they had a time of prayer I went forward to help the leader pray with more than a dozen who were kneeling at prayer stations.

The young man I came alongside was weeping hard, his shoulders shaking with sorrow. I asked if I could pray with and for him. He could barely speak. "I don't know how to say it . . . I just needed to do this."

I told him, "You know, you can just talk directly to God, right now, on your knees, out loud, and I'll hear it too. Then I'll know how to pray with you."

When churchy people pray out loud, it is often in a hushed voice so others can't overhear. This guy started praying out loud—very loud. "My life is so f—ed up, God. I've done all kinds of s—. I'm sorry." He got even more descriptive after that.

I was taken aback. I hadn't heard people use that kind of language in church before, much less in a direct prayer to God. My instinct was to tell him he really shouldn't talk to God that way. But for some reason I didn't stop him; perhaps it was just the shock. And I'm glad I didn't. That would have been like the Pharisees: unable to see the miracle before their eyes and shaming people for the technicality of carrying a mat on the Sabbath. If I had interrupted this man's sincere prayer, I would have become a Pharisee 2.0.

The young man charged forward in his colorful confession. He shared all kinds of weaknesses to sin. He didn't have any flowery words for God. He didn't have any deep theological terms. It was raw confession liberally sprinkled with cusswords. At one point I think he used a *dammit* for emphasis, and I smiled, thinking, "Now you're talking to the One who actually can damn things!"

As I think about that guy throwing himself on the mercy of God, I wonder how often we who are already in the church would push people like him away with our spiritual systems. We haven't made enough room for Jesus to show up and make broken people well. He doesn't fit into our neat religious system any better than do those we push away from the church. Perhaps we trust our system to save us instead of the Savior himself? A Savior who doesn't need the system to save threatens those of us who control the saving system. And we who control it need saving just as much as anyone.

We remember that the presence of Jesus brings miracle-moving grace to those who are stuck. We must look up from the place where we are stuck, whether it be physically or spiritually, see the Savior standing there, and answer, "Yes. Yes, Lord, I want to be well, and you're the only One who can make it so."

And he will look at us and say, "Get up! Pick up your mat and walk."

PRAYER

You are with me, Jesus. I have been hoping and praying that things would change for me. But I've felt stuck in place. I haven't known how to change that. To be honest, I have been relying on my own system to solve my problems. That hasn't worked yet. I realize that I need you to make me truly well. I am ready and want to be well. Thank you, Jesus, my healer!

FOR REFLECTION

1. Have you ever felt stuck in some way? What was that circumstance? Are you still in a similar situation?

2. Jesus asked the man, "Do you want to get well?" What are the signs that someone truly wants to get well? What are they willing to do? What are they paying attention to? Are these things true of you?

3. Read John 5:1–15. Notice how the man relied on a system that wasn't working to gain healing, and how he failed to realize that the One standing before him could heal him. What systems or habits do you rely on that might distract you from the presence of Jesus?

4. In what ways do you feel you are going through the motions in your spiritual life? What might give new life to these areas so you can experience the transforming presence of Jesus?

6

OVERWHELMED

JOHN 6:1–15

I was walking back to the church in Zambia. Holding my right hand was Mickey, and holding my left was his sister. I did not speak their language, nor they mine, yet as our group walked the several miles from their hut to the center of the nearest village, these two grabbed my hands.

We had just visited Mickey's entire family. His mother, father, and sister all had AIDS. Mickey had been spared this disease so far, but his entire family was dying. We later sponsored Mickey through Hope for Children, which is how I learned his name. That one sponsorship would provide enough money to buy the drugs that would keep his sister alive and allow his other siblings to attend school. It would also provide for his mother, who had not told the village of her condition, so she could continue to serve in the village, helping other families, especially AIDS orphans and other vulnerable children like her own.

On the way, Mickey and his sister talked to me and I talked to them, not understanding a word but fully understanding their hearts. We arrived at the church where their minister, Pastor Rose, delivered a sermon I didn't understand, though she clearly touched the crowd crammed into the mud-brick sanctuary. The nearest water supply for Mickey and his family lay the same distance in the opposite direction, a stream not safe for drinking. While I was there, a team from World Hope International tried to dig a well but came up dry.

Later, we drove the many bumpy miles back to the guesthouse in silence. While gathering in the comfortable living room, debriefing and praying with our group, we added up the number of orphans and vulnerable children we had taken responsibility for in four villages: 538. I wrote the number on a card and stared at it for a long time. Five hundred thirty-eight children whose parents had died of AIDS or were already afflicted with the disease, like Mickey's parents. Each of these children might contract AIDS themselves or see their parents die if we did not intervene. As in Mickey's case, these 538 represent two, three, or even more children who could benefit from just one child in their family being sponsored. We were responsible for *thousands*, and our resources didn't seem like enough.

I stared at that number, overwhelmed. And I wept.

We had left that village in Zambia without striking water, and I remembered the sight of the entire village surrounding the drilling rig as the crew began to drill—happy, expectant for hope to gush forth. A few days later when I arrived home, I took a walk with my children, holding their hands as Mickey and his sister had held mine. I still couldn't comprehend the immensity of the problem. We continue to sponsor Mickey, who is now a teenager, and his family. We contributed toward a new well, which was eventually completed. I hope we made a dent in the overwhelming problems Mickey and his village face. But as I think back on that visit, I'm still overwhelmed by the immensity of Mickey's situation and how privileged my own son is. I'm overwhelmed at the thought of Mickey's sister's fate, how different it is from the fate of my daughters, who were fortunate to have been born in a different world. Although we have the same calling and are ordained by the same denomination, I'm overwhelmed with the challenges of Pastor Rose's ministry and how different hers must be than mine. I came home and had to arrange for cleaning services at our 66,000-square-foot church building; her concern was procuring clean water for her people so they wouldn't get diseases.

Even now, years after that visit, I feel overwhelmed by all of this and weep again. I'll never get over that experience. I'm not sure I should.

AMONG SO MANY

Andrew felt something similar in John 6. He looked upon the "great crowd" (v. 2) and compared that to the few loaves and fishes the disciples had, their limited resources, and he was overwhelmed. He said what any of us would say: "How far will they go among so many?" (v. 9).

We ask a version of this question, all of us, from time to time: How far will what I have go?

Jesus had been attracting larger and larger crowds. His popularity was peaking because of the miracles. Thousands showed up to hear him speak and perform wonders. The problem on this day was that they had followed him into the countryside, and there was no food to be had. Jesus turned to Philip and asked him, "Where shall we buy bread for these people to eat?" (v. 5). John tips us off that Jesus had a plan: "He already had in mind what he was going to do" and this was "only to test" Philip (v. 6). You have to love that Jesus was essentially giving Philip a hard time. Jesus knew exactly the kind of guy Philip was, and he responded in kind: "It would take more than half a year's wages to buy enough bread for each one to have a bite!" (v. 7).

Every committee has a Philip on it. A Philip is someone who breaks out the calculator during the debate and dismantles the entire proposition before the brainstorming begins. The world is full of Philips who point out what won't work. Philip always cast things negatively. He could have said, "If we committed nine months' wages to this problem it might be enough." But no, Philip was a pessimist. He overestimated the need and underestimated the provision. Life is easier for pessimists, because when things don't work out they take consolation in the fact that they saw it coming, which is somehow reassuring to a Philip.

Andrew, however, was an optimist. He went searching for food and came back with a report. Unfortunately, this crowd was full of poor Galileans, and they weren't the types to have packed a lunch. They were hungry, oppressed people, living under the thumb of Roman rule. Andrew's reconnaissance mission returned only one sack lunch from a boy, containing five small loaves and two small fish. Even Andrew's pluck had its limit, as he mentioned that the loaves and fishes were both small (v. 9).

So Andrew was overwhelmed as he looked upon the crowd, trying to contemplate how in the world he and his fellow disciples would feed this great multitude of hungry people, far from home. Andrew would discover that the presence of Jesus offers unexpected provision for the overwhelmed.

HAVE YOU BEEN WITH JESUS?

Andrew had plenty of compassion; that wasn't the problem. Lack of effort wasn't the problem either. He had gone out to search for resources only to find that the only food available was a sack lunch some embarrassed boy's mother had insisted he bring along that day. Andrew's problem wasn't leadership. He was the only disciple taking initiative in the situation.

Andrew's problem was reality. It stared him in the face just as the crowd in that Zambian village stared at me, looking for water. Compassion wasn't enough to overcome the stark reality of that problem. Nor was this lunch enough to feed more than five thousand hungry people. Andrew had compassion and he had a lunch, but among so many, that was clearly not enough. I bet you often feel the same way Andrew felt looking at the crowd, and the way I felt looking at the crowd in Zambia.

"How far will it go?" Andrew asked. We all ask this. We have our lunch to offer, but how far will it go among so many.

We offer what we have and hope it makes a dent in things. I hope what my family is doing for Mickey makes a difference. But I know it can't help all that much. We can't change the whole situation for Mickey's family or for his village, much less all of Zambia. Some might even say that what we're doing causes more harm by creating dependency. Are they right? I don't know. I'm overwhelmed just thinking about it. Many people claim to have the solution for places like Zambia, and that other solutions are part of the problem. Yet the problem remains despite the varied efforts at a solution.

What happens when compassion is not enough to solve the problem? Usually we become desensitized to the problem. We get cynical. We expect less of others and ourselves. When we repeatedly contribute to solutions that produce no change, we start to wonder if it is worth the trouble. We develop compassion fatigue. When your heart aches because of a need but your mind is numbed by its scale, you too might be overwhelmed and on the verge of compassion fatigue.

When you see the vast number of unemployed, hungry, or poor and can no longer think of ways to help without feeling frustrated, you're overwhelmed. When you help people with their rent or electric bill and expect them to come back to the well next month for more help, you're overwhelmed. When you stand among so many trapped in generational patterns of dependency on alcohol, sex, or drugs, it deadens your senses.

We become either pessimists, like Philip, who distance ourselves from the problem, or optimists, like Andrew, who respond with compassion but are still overwhelmed with the situation that seems unlikely to change.

Before we talk about how to handle big problems in general, let's take a look at the lunch. Jesus took the boy's lunch, prayed, and multiplied it. It's the miraculous feeding of the five thousand. Jesus had the disciples distribute the food, then pick up the leftovers.

Your hunch about your lunch is accurate: It's not enough. Nothing you can possibly bring to the problem is enough to solve it. What you need is not a bigger lunch, or even more people to contribute their meager lunches. You don't need a better fund-raising strategy or better brochures and marketing campaigns. What you need is to give your lunch to Jesus. Because "what are they among so many" becomes "they had eaten their fill" when Jesus gets his hands on your resources. Start simply by offering what you have to Jesus.

DON'T LET THEM MAKE YOU KING

When Egyptologists visited the tomb of Ramesses II in 1974, they found that the mummy was quickly deteriorating. They flew the pharaoh's remains to Paris to take a deeper look. So, many thousands of years after the king of Egypt was laid to rest, he got a first-class flight to Paris. Interestingly, the Egyptian government issued Ramesses II a valid passport. Needing to specify an occupation, they put down "King (deceased)." When the mummified corpse of Ramesses II arrived, the French gave him full military honors, as they would any head of state.[1] This might be why they say, "It's good to be king." Even thousands of years after death, you continue to get the royal treatment.

It would be nice to be royal, wouldn't it? To be king for a day sounds kind of nice. Jesus had just that opportunity in John 6. After Jesus fed the crowd, his full-bellied fans start thinking they could get used to all this. These tired, poor, huddled masses got a full day of teaching and healings, with a free lunch on top of it. They hastily formed the Committee to Elect Jesus Christ King.

But Jesus declined to be made "king by force" (v. 15). *Poof!* He disappeared like a magician. In an instant, the most popular person in Galilee went missing. Imagine how hard that would be for anyone but the Son of God to accomplish. Could the president slip away during a parade without the Secret Service knowing? Could a rock star sneak out of his or her own concert? Could the MVP quarterback slip out of a parking lot filled with fans after the big game?

For Jesus, there would be no encore. He was not backstage, in the locker room, or in some secret compartment under the floor waiting for the right moment to reappear. As soon as the crowd wanted to make him king, he made a supernatural exit. By doing so, he illustrated two things: (1) what typically happens after you satisfy the masses, and (2) what to do about it.

After you help people solve a big problem, they typically want to make you king. When you meet needs, people will be grateful. They will put you on a pedestal. Those you lead through a tough season will begin to think you are the key to their future journey. While eating the food, the crowd didn't think much about where it came from. They thought only of their hunger. But with full stomachs, they looked around and realized a miracle had happened. And they responded with gratitude.

After getting through the rough patch, those to whom you have offered hope and help will feel they owe you one. When a celebrity does aid work, no one can resist turning it into a photo op, often even the celebrity. When you do good for others, they often want to honor you. They try to make you king. And Jesus has shown you what to do about it.

It is tempting to garner accolades after doing a good work in the world. You have worked so very hard. A little gratitude seems like a well-earned reward. So few people are grateful anyway, why not soak it up for once? Jesus' example shows us that we may smell the perfume of praise briefly but must beware of splashing it on. The odor will eventually reek and make you gag. Some people are glory sponges and suck it all in, never exhaling. Don't do this. Be cordial. Be gracious. Acknowledge the thanks of others. Then direct praise to God. If others orchestrate events so that you become a sort of idol, follow the example of Jesus and quickly make for the exit. Disciples of Christ disappear when the crowd wants to worship them.

You can always tell who is a glory sponge when they finally get praised. They have been waiting for it for a long time. All their hard work has finally paid off, and they bask in the admiration of others. But those more like Christ are uncomfortable with too much attention. They start to derail the coronation planning committee by pointing to Christ and self-deprecate their way to the second chair so that his glory increases and theirs decreases.

THE LEGEND OF THE STAR THROWER

If you have a good deal of compassion for others, you may be tempted to believe a myth. The myth is that it's about you. The legend is that you are the savior and everything depends on your effort. That myth is recounted in the legend of the star thrower.

According to this legend, an old man walks down to the beach at dawn. The tide has washed in starfish that are strewn across the sand as far as the eye can see — an endless number. A young man is on the shore vigorously grabbing starfish and tossing them back into the sea.

The old man, amused and curious, asks the young one, "Why?" The youth replies that the stranded starfish will dry out and perish in the morning sun if he doesn't throw them back. The older, wiser one says, "But the beach goes on for miles and there are thousands and thousands of starfish. How can your effort make any difference?"

The young man looks thoughtfully at the single starfish cradled in his hand. He throws it into the sea and says, "It made a difference to that one." And he continues the impossible task.

This story has been printed in dozens of books, told by hundreds of pastors, and posted on numerous blogs—I found more than a thousand with a simple Internet search. The moral of the story is that you should do your little bit, throw in as many starfish as you can, for it makes a difference to that *one*.[2]

A moment ago, I urged you to "offer your lunch," meaning to offer your resources, however small, to Jesus. Clearly there is nothing wrong with throwing starfish back—that is, trying to help individuals in the face of an overwhelming systemic problem. By all means, throw every starfish you come across back to the sea; give up all your loaves and fishes. But beware of believing the myth that solving the world's problems is all about you, that *you* are the savior. Before you conceive yourself as the reincarnation of the star thrower, remember two things.

First, remember that the biggest problems are always systemic. There may be larger forces at work in this fallen world that affect those in need, which would save even more starfish if you were to solve them. The tides that beach the millions can be altered only by large-scale changes in the system (think social injustice, for instance: human trafficking, immigration reform, or the wealth gap). Ask questions like, "Why are more starfish on the beach these days than there used to be?" Inquire of those older and wiser whether there are changes in the patterns. For instance, even though it makes my family feel better to help little Mickey, have I truly helped him until I've considered the global systems that perpetuate poverty in his country and poured energy into making macro-level changes? Star throwers dare not be so pleased by the satisfaction of saving a few for the short-term effort that they fail to question whether something more, something grander, might be done to create a bigger solution. Don't settle for being a solitary, star-throwing savior.

Second, remember that you are not a king. No one can make you king by force. In the end, all kings self-coronate. No one can turn you into an idol without your permission. Glory seekers must be willing to stand on the pedestal where others place them. But you won't do that. You won't make yourself king. You'll climb off the pedestal. If Jesus, who had every right to kingship, didn't let them make him king, you don't want to be king either.

So offer your lunch and throw starfish back, but remember you are not the Savior. Jesus is. You can't truly save anybody. You merely introduce them to the One who saves. You are the one who knows the Savior—nothing more and nothing less. You're not the king; you are his subject. You and I are unwise youths tossing marine life to the waves—mere children with meager loaves and fishes in a lunch sack—nothing more.

Do this not as a grand sacrifice to be honored for. Your help cannot sustain anyone without Christ's saving grace. Give out of generosity; serve out of faith. Start by offering your lunch, then watch it multiply.

JESUS MULTIPLIES

One day God told my friend Sia to take her entire paycheck and buy groceries for the local food bank. She showed up there unannounced with a trunk full of food and found their shelves almost entirely empty; they were sending people home hungry. The food bank workers brought out a shopping cart and took food inside, then came back for more. They did that another time, and then another. After several trips hauling full carts of the same size Sia had used just once at the store, she wondered what was happening. Then she realized, glorying in the miracle of God, he had multiplied the food in her trunk to feed hungry people. She had witnessed a modern-day miracle of multiplication.

Sia took this as a sign from God that she should do more than feed people that one day. She filled out an application, interviewed, and started working at the food bank. She had come to give away food but ended up giving away herself. She offered her lunch. God multiplied it on that day and has been ever since. The presence of Jesus offered unexpected provision for Sia when she was overwhelmed.

Left to yourself, your efforts will fall far short, but if you give them to Jesus, he will multiply them. Don't bail when the going gets tough; don't fret when the problem is too large. Don't let your heart become numb to the needs of the crowd. Sure, your little bit on its own is barely a drop in the Sea of Galilee, but Christ multiplies that lone drop into a ripple. Offer your lunch and let God multiply—this is his business. Don't get compassion fatigue. Just do what you can.

Jesus doesn't need much to make a miracle. No Herculean effort on your part is required, just a few loaves and fishes. Your small resources provide an opportunity for Jesus to prove that point. We think fewer resources mean less potential. We think less means *less*, and more means *more*. But Jesus thinks fewer raw materials make for a rarer miracle. For him, less always becomes more.

We like things big. We want big-screen TVs and extra large microwave dinners to eat in front of them. We want family-sized portions and super-sized fries. Why get large when extra large is available? Why settle for standard when extended is an option? To us, more means more.

Jesus is just the opposite. He seems oddly energized by the small. He is fascinated by the widow's one coin, not the rich man's trumpets. He is obsessed with the one lost lamb, not the ninety-nine in the pen. When he casts vision, he doesn't talk about big buildings, budgets, or how many butts will be in the seats. No, he talks about ordinary tiny things like mustard seeds and yeast germs. To our Lord, your lunch isn't small; you're offering the raw ingredients for the multiplied miraculous. To Jesus, less means more.

So when Andrew was overwhelmed and wondered how far the two loaves and five fishes would go "among so many," Jesus smiled and thought, "Oh, Andrew, I love you brother, but you haven't figured out that less means more to me. If we had a KFC on this corner, the Father would get no glory." OK, Jesus didn't literally think of fried chicken, but he did use this occasion to make that very point. Your lunch might be small, but Jesus can multiply it.

FOOD THAT ENDURES

Miracles such as the feeding the multitude in John 6 are what Lesslie Newbigin calls "signs pointing to a gift that is never exhausted, a satisfaction that never passes."[3] Jesus put a finer point on it, saying to the crowd, "Do not work for food that spoils, but for food that endures to eternal life, which the Son of Man will give you" (v. 27). The lesson for those of us overwhelmed by the never-ending need for compassion? Fill more than stomachs. Fill the holes in the souls of those you serve, for only Jesus can truly sustain their lives.

To offer hope without the Holy One is shortsighted and a cruel postponement of deeper need fulfillment. Marketing hope without providing the gospel is like spreading frosting on government cheese and calling it a cheesecake. It is a trick, a sleight of hand that fills a stomach or pays the rent but doesn't fill the soul or pay the penalty for sin. Only Christ can do that.

Of course, this isn't a choice between the two. Jesus does both. Jesus offers a free lunch along with "food" that sustains eternally. The work of Jesus includes both a food bank and a Bible study, and ours should as well. If we follow Christ's example, the "so many" seem like only a few, and those seeking another free lunch will be those who have had their fill in him.

Start by offering your lunch. Then watch it multiply. But seek the eternal.

PRAYER

You are with me, Jesus. That's good because I'm overwhelmed by what I see in the world today. I've been working so very hard, and now I know that I must offer you what few resources I have. I rely on you to multiply my efforts so that eternal results might follow. I know I'm not the savior, and I won't let them treat me as one, for you alone are the Savior, the King. Thank you, Jesus, my multiplier!

FOR REFLECTION

1. What problems in the world do you care deeply about? When did you realize that compassion is not enough to solve these problems? Have you felt overwhelmed by the "so many" problems around you?

2. Which of your resources seem too small to meet the needs you see? What is the "small lunch" you are offering to God to multiply? What would it look like if God did multiply your offering?

3. Read John 6:1–15. Do you relate most to overwhelmed Andrew, pessimist Philip, or the unsuspecting boy with the lunch in this situation?

4. What is the "food that endures" that God wants you to work toward? What is the bigger, eternal, spiritual problem that God wants to fix for the people whose needs you care about?

7
AFRAID

JOHN 6:16–21

You would think being an astronaut was enough to make you famous. However, not many of us knew the name Chris Hadfield until he shot a YouTube video on the International Space Station. Major Hadfield had trained for decades as a fighter pilot, scientist, and astronaut for his space-station work. While there, Hadfield shot a video of himself singing a perfect-pitch rendition of the David Bowie song "Space Oddity" as he and his guitar floated in a capsule in space. Millions watched the video, and it revitalized the song in the public consciousness. Bowie said it was the best cover of the song he had heard. After returning to Earth, Hadfield gave numerous interviews that included details about the oddities of space travel.[1]

Safely nestled aboard the cozy 150-billion-dollar station, Hadfield traveled 221 times faster than our seventy-miles-per-hour speed limit, clocking in at three and a half miles *per second*.[2] Orbiting the Earth sixteen times a day, the space-station inhabitants see a sunrise or sunset every forty-five minutes. Hadfield described it as the most beautiful human-inhabited place in the universe, having the best views of the earth possible.

Once, Hadfield was resting and looking out a window upon Australia at night, which is a beautiful sight from the space station because the major cities are on the coast, appearing like a string of shining diamonds in the dark. Hadfield related that it was one of the most smile-inducing and safest-feeling times aboard the craft. As he watched, a meteor entered Earth's atmosphere between the space station and Australia and burned for many seconds. He marveled, at first, at the beauty of it. Yet immediately afterward, he felt a sense of dread, realizing that if the meteor's path had taken it just a few miles in another direction, it would have hit the space station. Such an impact would have destroyed the station and all aboard, including himself.

This is a man who had conquered all kinds of fears as a fighter pilot on Earth, who left the planet by being launched into weightless space, then exited the safety of the craft for a soundless spacewalk, and later had the courage to cover a David Bowie song for all the world to hear—this man who treated the terrifying as routine was now deeply afraid because of one falling star.

Even those trained to overcome mind-boggling fears invariably still have a few that grip them tightly. And if we are honest, we too will admit that we are afraid.

I suspect that you feel afraid of something, and despite your best efforts, you know you're not as safe as you pretend to be. Don't worry, fear is the starting point for many of the lessons Jesus has to teach.

HAVE YOU BEEN WITH JESUS?

Jesus' training of the disciples in John 6 began at the point of fear. No teacher sharpens the senses and hones our focus like fear does. Jesus used the disciples' fear to bring them deeper into the ways of the faith. "When evening came, his disciples went down to the lake, where they got into a boat and set off across the lake for Capernaum. By now it was dark, and Jesus had not yet joined them. A strong wind was blowing and the waters grew rough. When they had rowed about three or four miles, they saw Jesus approaching the boat, walking on the water; and they were frightened" (vv. 16–19).

So how about you? Have your waters grown rough? Do you have your eyes set on the other shore but face strong winds? Some might look at the winds and the waves assailing your life and think little of them. Others may dismiss your trials because they overcame similar storms in their past. The storms tossing another's boat seem tame from the shore. The violence of a storm can be felt only from inside it. Sometimes winds push your sail in the wrong direction. Waves take you off course, and rains drench your dreams.

What storms do you fear most? Perhaps it's a difficult boss or an even more difficult spouse. For some it may be a disease or a potential traffic accident. For others it is an enslaving addiction. You might fear failure or perhaps the greater responsibility success might bring. You might feel the unwanted effects of discrimination, poverty, or lack of education that push back your efforts and the storm clouds swirl around you.

Even the translators of John 6 may have underplayed the storms the disciples faced. The wording in the original language is more potent than our English phrase "a strong wind was blowing." The wind was a violent, tempestuous wind.[3] It was a *megas* wind, and you probably don't need a Greek dictionary to realize that *megas* means "great" or "huge." You can't know how much fear you'll feel in the unexpected mega-storm until you're in it. The presence of Jesus for those struggling in the storm changes the way they see the storm, themselves, and even Jesus himself.

THE KNIFE'S EDGE

When I was a child, our family was not the beach-going or tourist-trap type. We shunned the crowds and went for the forest; we chose the mountains over the coasts and went canoeing instead of shopping. Most kids get video games, baseball gloves, or toys for Christmas. I got things like a canoe paddle, a sleeping bag, and a backpack.

Because of this outdoor obsession, my whole family, including my younger brother, who was just eight years old at the time, climbed

Mount Katahdin in Maine. It gets its name from a Native American word meaning "the greatest mountain." This mountain is the first or last stop on the Appalachian Trail, depending on which direction you hike. It is beautiful, picturesque, and exposed. On the final ascent to the summit, the trail is only three feet wide, with thousand-foot cliffs on either side. It's like walking on the edge of a knife. In fact, that trail is called Knife's Edge, and it cuts deep. In the last several decades, nineteen people have died on Katahdin, most from exposure or falls from the Knife's Edge.[4]

The weather didn't cooperate with our attempt to cross the Knife's Edge. With a few failed attempts already under our belt and time running out both on our permit and our calendar, we decided to try the summit one last time. It began to rain. Because of the unprotected nature of the ascent and the altitude, the wind snapped this way and that. We had some makeshift rain gear—but nothing like the high-tech equipment available today. We dragged our wet, cold bodies up the side of that mountain for hours on end, finally reaching the Knife's Edge. Clouds had rolled in and we couldn't see more than forty feet in front of ourselves. Every time we thought we had reached the top, we found it was a false summit, and the mountain would continue to rise, seemingly endless in its ascent, growing before our eyes as the storm pounded us into submission.

That's when my brother, John, started to shake. We gathered around him to see what was wrong. He was speechless, with blue lips protruding from a hood he had cinched around his nose and mouth. He was in trouble and we knew it. Dad explained that he was approaching hypothermia and we needed to find shelter quickly. But exposed as we were on the Knife's Edge, there was no rock big enough to hide us. We turned around and started down the same trail with a new goal before us: getting John to safety.

Down the trail, we found a cluster of boulders that formed a partial cave. We crawled into that space and huddled around John. We took off his coat, then put our coats (which our body heat had warmed) on him. His skin looked like blue death. We hugged together as a family, and my parents prayed he would be OK. I was deeply afraid for what might have been the first time in my life. Could my brother actually die right here on the trail? It seemed impossible. But looking at him, I could tell he was in desperate condition. The "greatest mountain" had taken dozens; could my brother be next?

He wasn't. John made it through this ordeal and hiked many times again, including several times with me in California, Austria, and Scotland. But I remember how it felt in that cave. I was so very afraid, huddled away against the storm we had walked into. Whenever I think of deep fear, I remember this episode on the mountain.

You may not take crazy vacations like my family did, and you may think we got what we deserved for taking such risks. You may dismiss my fear in your own way; that ordeal may seem reckless or even trivial, but I know what a storm feels like. I have felt deep, overwhelming fear.

We in the Western world spend all kinds of time and money to ensure our safety, but from time to time a shocking occurrence awakens our sense of danger. Violence sometimes reaches our protected shores—a child is abducted, a shooter is on the loose, or a terrorist cell is discovered. Sometimes our fears are more figments. In the absence of daily danger, we play up the possible ways we *might* be endangered, from potential toxins in our foods to prying villains invading our privacy. At times our fears are very personal, such as when a loved one lies dying. We are afraid even in a world we've constructed to keep us safe.

You might ask this question of yourself: Do I feel safe?

When our prized safety is threatened, we become afraid. And when we are afraid, like the disciples, we discover that our safety is at risk. Yet when we are honest about our fears, we learn to trust in the only true resource during a storm: Jesus.

WHAT FEAR DOES TO US

The whale ship *Essex* set sail from Nantucket in August of 1819 in search of whales in the Pacific Ocean. Captain George Pollard and his first mate, Owen Chase, became the inspiration for Captain Ahab and Mr. Starbuck in the novel *Moby Dick.*

By November 1820, they were thousands of miles west of the South American coast, near the equator, when they found a pod of whales, ripe for bloody harvest. One of the enormous whales, likely eighty to one hundred feet long, or as long as the *Essex* itself, turned upon the ship when one of the younger whales was attacked with harpoons. This was a strange occurrence, recorded only one other time in history. The giant whale charged the ship, striking the hull, first mate Owen Chase recounted, coming "down upon us at full speed, [and striking] the ship with his head, just forward of the fore-chains; he gave us such an appalling and tremendous jar, as nearly threw us all on our faces. The ship brought up as suddenly and violently as if she had struck a rock, and trembled for a few seconds like a leaf."

The whale circled back, and after regaining himself, came "down apparently with twice his ordinary speed, and with tenfold fury and vengeance in his aspect."

The ship was lost. All twenty of the crewmembers abandoned the whaling ship to the smaller whaleboats, grabbing what supplies they could.

After gathering themselves and taking stock, they found they had six pounds of hard bread, three casks of water, a musket, powder, and tools. Oddly enough, a crewmember had brought a few turtles. They may have started out as pets, but they would surely be soup before long.

After surveying their maps, the crew found that they had few options, being so far from any land in the Pacific. They had food enough for sixty days of sailing. The Marquesas Islands were to the west, and they could certainly make it there. Hawaii was to the north, and they might make it there if they could stretch their provisions. Chile was to the east, thousands of miles away, with the winds and current against them.

The Marquesas Islands were the obvious choice, but the crew was gripped by a rumor that the islands were inhabited by cannibals, the oft-exaggerated boogeyman of that era. Hawaii made the next best choice. But the captain was sure there would be storms between their location and Hawaii at that time of the year. So rather than choosing any of the more logical options before them, they determined to turn their three longboats south, toward Antarctica, in hopes of catching a current eastward toward Chile. There was no chance, given their stores and the distance, of making it in time. Yet rather than conquer their fear of storms and cannibals, the crew set off for Chile.

The crew of twenty that had fled in terror of savages became savage themselves. Months later, a passing ship found the eight surviving crewmembers, discovering men who had themselves become cannibals. From grisly experience, they had calculated that three men could live for seven days on one human corpse.[5]

I told this stunning and gruesome story to my kids on the way to church on a Sunday morning when I knew we would be talking about fear. I asked them what they thought the moral of the story was. My eleven-year-old daughter said, "The moral of the story is 'Go to Hawaii!'" I agree. If I have to choose between eating, being eaten, or sailing through a typhoon, I would choose the storm any day.

My thirteen-year-old son may have summed up the moral best when he said, "Be careful what you do with your fears, or you may become what you fear." Our fears can indeed consume us. Never one to pass up the chance for dark comedy, Max ruined this wonderfully wise moment by adding, "Another moral to the story is 'You are what you eat!'"

Matthew 14 describes the same scene depicted in John 6. Matthew says the wind was tossing them about, using a word meaning "distressed" or "harassed," even "torture" or "pain."[6] Ironically, Mark 6 describes this same episode using a phrase often translated "straining at the oars." This is the same as used in Matthew 14. The storm harassed them into harassing themselves because of fear.

Isn't this often the case? Fear starts as a natural, even healthy, response. But it grows to the point that we torture ourselves with it. Fear is real, and fear is needed. We cannot wish away fear, nor should we. Yet when fear paralyzes us or pushes us to distress, to "straining about the oars" rather than trusting God, fear has gotten the better of us. As the crew of the whale ship *Essex* learned, what we have to fear is not fear itself but what fear does to us.

WHOM DO YOU FEAR?

The first step to being honest about your fears is to realize what you are afraid of. It is helpful to write a list of the things that make you afraid. You might find that a few of them can be overcome easily. Others will take a strategic effort to defeat. Still others may stay with you a very long time.

I wonder if this name might be on your list of fears, whether you're aware of it or not: Jesus.

That's right. I think you might be afraid of Jesus. Before you dismiss this idea, hear me out. In churchy circles, we talk about Jesus with such flowery, wonderful words that it makes me wonder if we are concealing the fact that we are more distant from him than we care to admit. We don't feel true intimacy with Jesus. We may feel a sense of gratitude, surely; desire, probably; hope, even. But are we close to Jesus? Remember that this is God we're talking about. This is the guy who not only walks on water, but also calms the storms that toss us about.

And deep down, we understand that the One who has the power to calm storms can start them too. When uncontrollable storms are raging about us, it's hard to relate to the One who controls them. In fact, we may fear him. This is important to realize, for there is no greater barrier to intimacy than fear.

Those who are afraid of Jesus are in good company; the disciples feared him too. In John 6:19, the story continues as the disciples rowed against the wind and waves: "When they had rowed about three or four miles, they saw Jesus approaching the boat, walking on the water; and they were frightened."

This word *frightened* means "terrified."[7] The disciples were filled with terror at this apparition on the water. The storm still raged around them, but the disciples feared the strange one who could take a Sunday stroll through it. If we are honest, we'll admit such fear in ourselves as well. The presence of Jesus—for those of us struggling in the storm—changes the way we see the storm, ourselves, and even Jesus.

I AM

Jesus told us not to fear. On what basis? In verse 20, we see that he didn't just say, "Don't be afraid." He preceded that by saying, "It is I." Or, more accurately, "I AM; don't be afraid."

This statement rests on the identity of Jesus. He doesn't just tell us not to fear; he reminds us we don't need to fear because of *who he is*.

Jesus told the disciples his true identity while walking on the Sea of Galilee (as if walking on the water itself didn't answer the identity question already). When he said, "I AM" in the original language, this was a reference to all kinds of interesting history about the identity of God. What's more, to the original hearers—the men in the boat tossed about by the storm—this was understood as a claim by Jesus of his divinity.

Let's take a look at the big picture by surveying the early books of the Bible. The first time anyone asked God his name, this was his reply: "I AM." Sort of an odd thing to say, isn't it? Imagine meeting someone for the first time, and you say, "My name is Julie. What's your name?" And in return she says, "I always have been." Or maybe she says, "I will always be me." You might think she was a bit of a nut. But that's how God answered.

When Moses asked God for his name in Exodus 3, the encounter was accompanied by bush burning rather than water walking. But Jesus made clear to the disciples privately that he was not merely a king, a prophet, a teacher, or even a miracle worker. He is the "I AM" who had been introducing himself to the chosen ones, either in deserts (Ex. 6) or in captivity (Zech. 8:8), for centuries.

Throughout the Gospels, Jesus referred to himself with the words *I am*. He did this at least eight times in the book of John alone:

- "I am the bread of life" (6:35, 48).
- "I am the light of the world" (8:12; 9:5).
- "Before Abraham was born, I am" (8:58).
- "I am the gate" (10:9).
- "I am the good shepherd" (10:11).
- "I am the resurrection and the life" (11:25).
- "I am the way and the truth and the life" (14:6).
- "I am the true vine" (15:1).

Jesus defined himself. He is not merely a teacher; he is the one about whom teachers teach. He does not merely perform miracles; he is a miracle. Later in John 6, when Jesus spoke to the crowd chasing after him for bread, he gave them a strange reply, stating that he is not merely the baker, he is the bread.

Jesus is not merely a prophet either; he is the one about whom prophets prophesy. He is not merely one in a long succession of kings; he is the King of Kings, Lord of Lords. He is the "I AM."

Throughout the book of John, people wondered who Jesus was. The identity of Jesus was perhaps the key question for any gospel writer, particularly this one. In John 6 alone, there are at least four guesses at the identity of Jesus:

A. Was he a miracle worker (vv. 11, 19)?
B. Was he a prophet (v. 14)?
C. Was he a king (v. 15)?
D. Was he a teacher (v. 25)?

Correct answer? E: none of the above. Or, more accurately, he is more than the sum all these things. Prophet, king, teacher, miracle worker: these are roles Jesus might fulfill, but no single one can adequately describe him. Lesslie Newbigin may have said it best: "To say 'Jesus is king' is true if the word 'king' is wholly defined by the person of Jesus; it is false and blasphemous if Jesus is made instrumental to a definition of kingship derived from elsewhere. Jesus has come 'to proclaim liberty to the captives,' but he will not become the mascot for a people's movement of liberation. At the very moment when the cry 'Make Jesus king' is rending the air Jesus abruptly disappears."[8]

Jesus will not be defined by worldly occupations. We simply can't contain him. The closest we might come in describing his identity is to point to the family relationships within the Trinity. God is the Father. Jesus is the Son, namely, the Son of the Father God. "Everyone who has heard the Father and learned from him comes to me. No one has seen the Father except the one who is from God; only he has seen the Father" (vv. 45–46). And the Son will again "ascend to where he was before" (v. 62): with the Father.

Quite simply, Jesus is God. Why does the book of John spend so much time talking about the identity of Jesus? Because you'll never really know who you are until you truly know who Jesus is.

FEAR OF GOD

Perhaps now we should pause and note that to fear God is not only a natural thing, but is an honorable thing as well. The Bible indicates that the fear of the Lord is a virtue. However, the meaning of *fear* in that sense is closer to our word *awe* than to the terror the disciples felt in the boat. Yet having a healthy fear of God might be a good thing. Ambrose Redmoon said, "Courage is not the absence of fear, but rather the judgment that something else is more important than fear."[9] Our awe and worship of God is more important than the things that threaten us and make us afraid. And we dare not become so casual about Jesus that we lose respect for him. It is not shameful to fear God, for as Samuel Johnson said, "Shame rises from the fear of men, conscience rises from the fear of God."[10] Our intimacy with Jesus does not diminish his water-walking and storm-silencing power. It would be odd if we did not fear God at all.

Our problem, however, is that we often fear God so much that we don't invite him into the boat. We may be so terrified of God's power that we think of his presence as the problem. If God is the ghostly apparition walking through our storms and silencing them in his own good time, then he never becomes *our* Lord; he remains a distant God. Of course, he is God either way, even when we enter into relationship with him.

Fear paralyzes, as anyone who has frozen still upon seeing a snake or standing before an audience knows. It could be that a paralyzing fear of intimacy with the Creator keeps us from inviting Jesus into the boat. And it could be that we don't invite him in because we actually prefer noisy storms to the silence and peace he brings. Perhaps we fear what the silence might say. The all-powerful One is also all-knowing. It's one thing to get chummy with someone who controls the weather; it's another thing for him to know everything we ever did while he says, "Be still."

While a healthy fear (or awe) of God is OK, living in constant fear is not. In fact, Jesus repeatedly tells us not to be afraid.

THE MOST COMMON COMMAND OF CHRIST

One of my joys in life is working as the personal researcher for Max Lucado, the best-selling author and pastor from San Antonio, Texas. He is an amazing writer and has taken me under his wing through the last decade of working for him. Max often gets a hunch about something in Scripture, sometimes in unexpected ways.

Once he told me that he was interested in writing on the subject of fear. He was concerned that people seemed to be more and more afraid these days, and were trapped by those fears. He said he had a hunch that the most common command of Jesus was "Do not fear."

I was skeptical upon hearing this (and it's my job to be). "Couldn't be true," I thought. "Certainly God commanded us to love, or serve, or be unified, or any number of other things more than to not fear." So I started crunching the texts.

I started with the Christ-issued imperatives in the Gospels, more than one hundred of them, and categorized them. I was astonished to discover that Max was right. (I'll confess to you that it's a little annoying how often his hunches are correct.) Max treated the subject of fear exceptionally well in his book *Fearless*.[11] I commend it to you as a next step after reading this chapter if it strikes a nerve about fear.

Twenty-one commands of Christ urge us to not be afraid or to not fear, or to have courage, take heart, or be of good cheer. While the latter commands don't mention the word *fear*, they have the same intent as those that do. As you might have guessed, the second most frequent command is to love—each other, God, even our enemies. If quantity is any indicator of importance, Jesus takes our fears seriously. The one command he gave more than any other was this: Don't be afraid. Even taking the most liberal translation of *love* and the most limited translation of *fear*, the latter still outpaces the former.[12]

Jesus tells us to not fear or worry but to have courage instead. Jesus takes fear very seriously, and seeks to help us overcome it. It makes sense, because "perfect love drives out fear" (1 John 4:18)!

JESUS IN YOUR BOAT

John 6 continues: "Then they were willing to take him into the boat, and immediately the boat reached the shore where they were heading" (v. 21).

Now the question remains: Is Jesus in your boat, or does he just walk on water in your world? Is he a spectral presence who does random miracles? Do you believe he exists "out there," ghostlike but never truly with you, only hovering around the edges of your life? Or have you invited Jesus into your boat?

We need a Christ who does more than walk on water. The real miracle Jesus wants to perform in your life is not walking on water or even calming storms. It is transforming your life entirely by stepping into your boat—so you no longer fear him but trust him. Admitting your fear of God and inviting Jesus into your boat enables you to face the real fears of life, to have courage, and to take heart.

Jesus often calms a stormy soul before he calms the storm itself. So take your eyes off the storm and look to the One who has the power to clear both the storms in your life and the clouds in your soul.

PRAYER

You are with me, Jesus. It is hard for me to admit what I'm afraid of. Most people think I have it pretty well together. But you know what I'm afraid of. In some ways, I'm even afraid of you. Show me your love, Jesus, and that I have nothing to fear, from you or this world. Thank you, Jesus, my peace!

FOR REFLECTION

1. Name something you are afraid of that seems silly even to mention. Now name something you fear more deeply, something that is difficult to talk about out loud.

2. What fears do you have that might put you in danger of becoming what you fear?

3. Read John 6:16–21. Jesus commands, "Do not be afraid" many times in Scripture. Is this an easy command for you to follow or a hard one? Why? What helps you cope with your fears?

4. In what ways does being with Jesus bring up fears you might not know you had?

8

GUILTY

JOHN 8:1–11

Louisiana, Florida, and South Carolina are guilty of the sin of wrath. Do you think I'm being judgmental on these southern states? Well, you should also know that West Texas and the greater Washington, DC, area are guilty of gluttony. And I should add that the areas surrounding San Francisco, Seattle, and Portland are guilty of envy. You might not be surprised to learn that Las Vegas is guilty of greed, but so are half the counties in California, Florida, and Arizona, as well as *every* county in *every* state from Maryland to Massachusetts. Los Angeles and several counties in Oregon, Montana, and Pennsylvania are guilty of sloth. Oh, and Mississippi, as a whole, is guilty of lust.

Perhaps you're worried that I'm pronouncing them sinful, but understand that these are not merely my opinions. These are plain facts. How can I make these claims? Researchers at Kansas State University used demographic data to create maps that tell Americans a lot about the proclivities of their hometowns.[1] They assessed the geographic incidence of violent crimes (murder, assault, rape) to determine which angry places are guiltiest of wrath. The places with highest reported theft counted for envy. Those with the highest per capita fast food restaurants got chalked up to gluttons, and the highest per capita sexually transmitted diseases got listed for lust. If you live in the United States, you will likely find that your county is listed among the sinners for one misdeed or another.

Labeling someone a sinner makes us uncomfortable. Even when a secular state university produces that finding based on demographic data, I still shy away from calling people sinners. The very word makes most of us uncomfortable.

SINNERS

The Pharisees and teachers of the law in Jesus' day didn't shy away from this at all. They were good at drawing lines in the sand to define sin. If our culture has a tendency to avoid calling anyone a sinner, their culture flipped the coin to the other side. The Pharisees labeled all kinds of people as sinners. Before being too judgmental of the Pharisees, we should remind ourselves that sin is a common subject in Scripture, and the word is used throughout the Bible. We often think the Pharisees and teachers of the law made up rules to alienate people arbitrarily, but they were merely trying to live up to *the* law, God's law found in the Scriptures. Following the many laws in Scripture was difficult to do and sometimes required what seems to us like strange behavior.

Imagine for a moment trying to abide by every law in the Old Testament. Slip into some Pharisee sandals for a stroll. You know that cotton-polyester blend shirt you have? It has to go because of Leviticus 19:19. Ever see your neighbors unloading a trunk full of groceries and fail to help them? I'm pretty sure you disobeyed Exodus 23:5. If you've ever walked by a homeless person and ignored their open hand, you broke the law according to Deuteronomy 15:7 and 24:19–20. If you've ever refused to give your spouse sex, then you broke the direct command of Exodus 21:10. And by the way, fellas, if your married brother died and didn't have children, you need to marry his widow and get her pregnant according to Deuteronomy 25:5.

If you went through all 613 laws found in the Torah (the first five books of the Old Testament), you'd find quite a few that you've broken—which just goes to show that you are a sinner. A few examples:

- Ever send email on a Saturday? You're a sinner (Ex. 20:10).
- Like lobsters? That makes you a sinner too (Lev. 11:9).
- Do you shave or trim your sideburns? Sorry, sinner (Lev. 19:27).
- Got a mortgage on your house? Yep, that's sinful too (Deut. 23:20).
- Lustful thoughts? Sinner (Num. 15:39)!
- Got tattoos? Sinner (Lev. 19:28)!
- Not tithing? Sinner (Lev. 27:30; Num. 18:24)!
- Do you enjoy eating bacon? Sorry to break it to you, but you are a big-time, greasy-crispy, bacon-loving sinner (Deut. 14:8).

A. J. Jacobs famously tried to live by all the laws of the Torah and recorded the effort in his book *The Year of Living Biblically*.[2] He found the commands to be taxing. The trickiest one involved his wife and Leviticus 15:19–20: "When a woman has her regular flow of blood, the impurity of her monthly period will last seven days, and anyone who touches her will be unclean till evening. Anything she lies on during her period will be unclean, and anything she sits on will be unclean."

Jacobs interpreted that to mean that he couldn't sit anywhere his wife sat during this, well, delicate time of the month. To spite him and this effort, his wife would sit on every chair in the house so that he would have to stand all day or carry a chair with him all the time.

Suffice it to say that following the law was exacting. Few, if any, of us would be able, even if willing, to follow all of these laws. By the time of Jesus, the Pharisees and teachers of the law wore a *tallit*, which is a prayer shawl even larger than the ones you might see some devout Jews wearing today. It might have been as long as a bed sheet. Six hundred thirteen fringes were added to this, representing each and every law, including the ones I referenced above, and, in fact, fulfilling the law found in Numbers 15:37–39.

These Pharisees and teachers of the law were good at keeping the law. They had it down to a science, always giving the right answer to each question. Jesus seemed to challenge their system at every turn. So they orchestrated a showdown.

HAVE YOU BEEN WITH JESUS?

Jesus showed up "again in the temple courts, where all the people gathered around him, and he sat down to teach them" (John 8:2). He began to teach the people, and the showdown with the religious leaders began when they "brought in a woman caught in adultery. They made her stand before the group" (v. 3).

You've already put yourself in the sandals of the Pharisees. Now take off those sandals and follow the barefoot walk of shame this woman took from her love nest to the temple courts. It is one thing to be guilty of sin and confess; it is another to be caught by accusers.

Often my wife walks briskly through our kitchen only to find me with my hands (and sometimes my entire head) inside the refrigerator, searching for ice cream. If I catch on quickly enough, I emerge with carrots. Often she catches me red-handed with the rocky road.

Getting your hand caught in the proverbial cookie jar, or in my case, the ice-cream bucket, can be a far more serious thing. An accountant is caught embezzling money from a Christian school. A schoolteacher is caught disciplining her students inappropriately. A church staff member catches the pastor in adultery. Sometimes catching someone in a sin causes a meltdown, a cascading destruction of jobs, families, reputations, and ministries. Most infractions lie somewhere between swiping sweets and swiping millions. What about getting caught on social media at work when you aren't supposed to be? Or swiping office supplies from the storeroom? How about charging personal items to your company account?

I'm not asking if you've ever done something wrong. You have.

I'm wondering if you've ever been caught.

Getting caught changes the dynamics of sin. When you feel guilty for sin, you may feel like a fraud. The worst part is knowing that your sin will eventually be discovered. Surprisingly, you might even *hope* someone will find out just so you can end the cycle of lying.

We all have guilt. We don't do the things we want to do, and we do the things we wish we could avoid (see Rom. 7:15–20). We may look at the sin in our lives and wonder how long it can last. We wonder if we can sustain things at their current trajectory, or if even our little sins will catch up to us too. So the question of this chapter, and of our lives, is this: What do we do about our sin? The presence of Jesus transforms the way we see sin in our lives and offers hope for change.

The woman caught in adultery knew her sin had found her out. She was dragged into the public square to face judgment. Her sin had brought her to a dead end.

GUILTY AS CHARGED

As I've gotten to know Dana Antal, his story has amazed me. I've heard some of it from him directly in conversation and some of it through stories in the press. His story includes many highs and lows in one life.[3]

As a fourth grader, Dana found a six-pack of beer under a cellar door on the way to school, and that discovery led to one addiction:

alcohol. Before long, he made his first bet, won a dollar, and thus began his second major addiction: gambling. He may have been one of the few to bet not only on the Olympic games but also on Nintendo games. In time, he would skip school to go to the track to feed his habit. Before he left his childhood home in Queens, New York, he had started a bookmaking operation in his bedroom.

Things escalated, and Dana became part of a vast network of crime. The district attorney described it as "a highly sophisticated criminal enterprise controlled by the Bonanno organized crime family." They oversaw illegal betting on baseball, football, and horse racing. The operation handled 360 million dollars.

Dana recalls, "Many times I owed money to the wrong people." One of these wrong people was a bookie with an "enforcer" who once cornered Dana and instructed him to put his hands on a table. Next, the enforcer took out a meat cleaver and said, "For every week you don't pay me, I will cut one of your fingers off." Lucky for Dana, he kept his fingers by borrowing ten thousand dollars from someone else to pay off the bookie.

By the age of twenty-seven, Dana says, "I felt dead inside. One night I got on my knees and said, 'God, there has to be something more than what I'm experiencing. Please show me.' The next day I experienced the overwhelming sense of peace and the embrace of his love. I called some friends and said I need to stop." Next came rehab, where Dana met a crack addict who later became his wife: LeeAnn. He also met a preacher and started to read the Bible, but Dana wasn't fully changed. He still gambled, and took bets from others.

He tried to escape that life by moving to Pennsylvania and severing ties with organized crime. He thought he had left the sin business behind, but two state troopers showed up at his house to take him back to New

York. He was charged with corruption enterprise, and bail was set at one million dollars. Dana made the cover of the New York *Daily News*.

At that point, Dana faced a choice: He could either fight the charges or plead guilty. That's when he found out that someone he barely knew from the church he had begun attending had put up their million-dollar property to make his bail, freeing him until his court date. Humbled and gripped in grace, Dana pled guilty to the charges.

Incarcerated at Rikers Island and, later, Attica, Dana studied the Bible. "I began to see myself for what I truly was: a criminal. I couldn't grasp how I could be a follower of God and be involved in the gambling world. . . . I began to realize I had a part to play in the destruction of people's lives," Dana said. He also began to realize God did not want to condemn him, but to change him.

After being paroled, Dana says he "began to really seek humility in a way that said I want to do whatever God wants me to do." He started a Gamblers Anonymous group, and also led a biblically based twelve-step program for people struggling with anger, depression, codependency, abuse, and addiction.

"I began to share my story without shame, guilt, or fear. People reacted with love and acceptance. If we take the mask off and allow ourselves and others to see the real us, we experience God's and man's love beyond measure."

Where is Dana now? After working with so many broken people, he felt called to the ministry. After years of study, he is now an ordained minister and colead pastor at a vibrant and diverse church, filled with people recovering from all kinds of addictions and seeking Christ's way.

All of this began in that moment when Dana realized he was guilty of the sin he stood accused of.

He decided to plead guilty. Have you?

You may not be a bookie and you may not have been caught in adultery, but have you lived up to all 613 commands? I know I haven't. I know I am guilty. If there are two camps—the perfect and the sinners—I'll stand with the bookie, addict, and the woman caught in adultery.

WOMAN CAUGHT

The woman stood, disheveled, at the center of the crowd. Her makeup had run down her face, smeared by tears. Her clothing was torn, and she frantically pulled at the shredded fabric in a vain attempt to protect herself from the eyes that both judged her and secretly lusted for her.

The Pharisees and teachers of the law said to Jesus, "Teacher, this woman was caught in the act of adultery. In the law, Moses commanded us to stone such women. Now what do you say?" (John 8:4–5).

What do you say?

Over dinner with my family, we discussed an obscure Bible passage found in Deuteronomy 21. My son, Max, was thirteen years old, his younger sister Karina was eleven, and Lauren was eight. I read the passage from the days of the exodus: "If a man has a stubborn and rebellious son, which will not obey . . . and they shall say unto the elders of his city, this our son is stubborn and rebellious, he will not obey our voice. . . . And all the men of his city shall stone him with stones, that he die" (Deut. 21:18, 20–21 KJV).

After a bit of silence Karina asked, "So does this mean you have to take Max to the nursing home and the old people would hit him with stones till he dies?"

We elected not to do that, using lesser punishments, when called for, mostly restricting the time Max could play video games, which seemed as painful for him as stoning might be.

Karina had lumped Max into the category "such teenagers," described in Deuteronomy 21. She labeled him a sinner (which never goes over well with siblings, does it?). In the case of the woman in John 8, the Pharisees and teachers of the law used a similar phrase: They said "such women" (v. 5) are to be stoned. We don't know the name of the woman. It may have been Sarah, Elizabeth, Mary, or something else. No one knows. So I call her the "woman caught." Her identity is wrapped up in her sin, which is a critical problem for all sinners. In fact, it may be *the* critical problem of our day.

In our struggles to preserve our rights and maintain our independence from one another, we equate the identity of persons with their actions, even, and perhaps especially, when those actions are sinful. So we may, without fully realizing it, accept a label someone else invented for us, which then becomes our "people group." This is what happened to the woman caught. She is known only by her sin. She was one of "such women." That is, until she met Jesus. He saw beyond the labels, as verse 6 makes clear: "They were using this question as a trap, in order to have a basis for accusing him. But Jesus bent down and started to write on the ground with his finger."

The religious leaders asked Jesus a direct question: Moses tells us to stone her; what do you say? But Jesus never answered the question. In fact Moses *did* tell them to stone her. But they knew Jesus always hung out with sinners. His compassion for them seemed to be more than they could stomach. So the question put Jesus between a rock and a hard place, and that's right where they wanted him.

They say you should never wrestle with a pig, because you just get dirty and the pig enjoys it. Jesus doesn't wrestle with the pigs on this one (which would not be Kosher anyway according to Lev. 11:4). Instead, he wrote in the sand. We don't know what he wrote. John didn't record it. Perhaps it was the sins of the accusers or their names. Like the name of the woman caught, Jesus' words have been lost to history.

After a few moments, the scene became awkward for the onlookers. Jesus was dodging the question. So they went after him again to force an answer. That's when "he straightened up and said to them, 'Let any one of you who is without sin be the first to throw a stone at her.' Again he stooped down and wrote on the ground" (John 8:7–8).

For those of us who know this story well, it is easy to rush past the fact that Jesus just gave the group permission to stone the woman. Yet he added a caveat, which was brilliant, a radical approach to sin and guilt. Rather than play along with the usual assumption that accusers are righteous and the accused are guilty, Jesus forced everyone with a stone in their hand—then and now—to examine themselves. This would be a good time for you to do the same.

Jesus positions us all in the sinner camp. He clarifies what Paul summarized in Romans 3:23: "For all have sinned and fall short of the glory of God." Jesus knows what all of us need to continually relearn: Only sinners get forgiven, so admitting that you are one is the best place to start.

I'll say it again: *Sinner* is not an exclusive club. Sinners are not members of a select group. We are all sinners. Although I poked a bit of fun at the "sinfulness" of different states at the beginning of this chapter, every person in every state and every province in every country, including you and me, is a sinner. The dividing line in history is not between sinners and non-sinners; it is between lost sinners and sinners saved by grace.

Jesus' risky tactic, walking the delicate line of grace that stands between harsh judgment and weak permissiveness, worked: "At this, those who heard began to go away one at a time, the older ones first, until only Jesus was left, with the woman still standing there" (John 8:9). The Pharisees lost something in this encounter and gained something at the same time. They lost their battle to make Jesus look bad. Their trap was sprung, but it failed to catch Jesus. Instead, they gained the realization that they had no right to throw stones. We can say this, at least, of the oft-derided Pharisees: When forced to state by their deeds whether they were sinners or sinless, their actions told the truth. They walked away, with a hint of grace no doubt working its way into their hearts.

Then "Jesus straightened up and asked her, 'Woman, where are they? Has no one condemned you?'" (John 8:10). Jesus was playing coy. Now that he had dealt with the accusers, he began to deal with the accused. He knew full well what had happened. He knew all that was transpiring in that court, including what the woman was feeling. She had narrowly escaped an early grave beneath a pile of stones and received an early parole with a heart of gratitude.

THE TRANSFORMING POWER OF FORGIVENESS

The woman caught had been looking for Mr. Right in all the wrong places. She finally found him in this strange Jesus, who dodged questions and answered his critics by drawing in the sand, driving off her accusers.

The woman only had one line in the story. She replied to the question of the Christ with this: "No one, sir" (v. 11).

"'Then neither do I condemn you,' Jesus declared. 'Go now and leave your life of sin'" (v. 11). She was forgiven. She not only met a man called Jesus, she met a Savior and Lord.

Notice that Jesus didn't say, "Nobody has a right to condemn you." In reality, Jesus could have condemned her himself by the laws of Scripture and of the universe. He could have picked up a stone and killed her himself. "He who is without sin . . . throw a stone . . . first" (v. 7 NKJV). That's a description of only *one* man, and he fit it perfectly. Jesus was a rabbi who wore a tallit with those fringes to remind him of the 613 laws; and he had lived up to every one of those laws. Any other rabbi would have been counting out each fringe that he had infringed upon. But Jesus never had to repent, never had to confess. He is sinless. The One without sin does have the right to condemn, but he also has the right and the power to forgive. This is grace. Jesus chose the way of redemption over the way of condemnation for the woman caught. And aren't we glad he chooses redemption over condemnation with us? The presence of Jesus transforms the way we see sin in our lives and offers hope for change.

Jesus also didn't say, "Now, go and when you sin remember I don't condemn you." Go ahead and read it. He said something that might be hard for us to accept: "Go and stop sinning." Some translations say, "Go now and leave your life of sin" or "Go and sin no more" (NLT, NKJV). Pastors often close a service with a benediction of flowery words beginning with, "Now, go." I've never heard one of them choose this benediction: "Go and stop sinning." However, I bet there are a few Sunday afternoon church board meetings where this would be the most helpful instruction.

What do we do with this command of Jesus? It doesn't fit into our contemporary view of sin, does it?

STOP IT

Bob Newhart is one of the great comedians of our age. His television shows and sketches are legendary. He came out of semiretirement to join a sketch with the younger cast of a newer TV show and pretty much showed them how it was done. It begins with psychiatrist Dr. Switzer, played by Newhart, talking to a new client, Katherine.

Switzer says, "Tell me about the problem that you wish to address."

Katherine replies, "I have this fear of being buried alive in a box. I just start thinking about being buried alive and I begin to panic."

After a series of follow-up questions Switzer and Katherine agree that she is claustrophobic. The doctor then moves very quickly to his prescription: "All right. Well, let's go, Katherine. I'm going to say two words to you right now. I want you to listen to them very, very carefully. Then I want you to take them out of the office with you and incorporate them into your life."

Katherine says, "OK."

Dr. Switzer then calmly says, "OK. Here they are." And then he yells, "Stop it!"

Befuddled, Katherine asks, "I'm sorry?"

Dr. Switzer then just repeats "Stop it!" over and over again, and after getting pushback he says, "You know, it's funny. I say two simple words and I cannot tell you the number of people who say exactly the same thing you are saying. I mean, you know, this is not Yiddish, Katherine. This is English. Stop it!"

Katherine tries to relate. "So I should just stop it?"

"There you go. I mean, you don't want to go through life being scared of being buried alive in a box, do you? I mean, that sounds frightening."

"It is."

"Then stop it," the doctor exclaims.

Katherine then mentions a few other problems she has, each one resulting in the same short, harsh directive from Dr. Switzer.

She's bulimic. Stop it, you kook!

She reads her horoscope. Stop it, weirdo!

She has problems with her mother. Stop it, silly!

Her relationships with men are destructive. Stop it! Stop it! Stop it!

After hearing all this, Katherine finally reaches her limit. She tells the doctor, "You stop it! You stop it!"

Seemingly surprised, he asks, "What's the problem, Katherine?"

"I don't like this," she replies. "I don't like this therapy at all. You are just telling me to stop it."

He surmises that they are moving too fast, and so he offers an alternative. "Let me give you ten words that I think will clear everything up for you."

Katherine gets out a pad and a pencil to take notes.

"Are you ready?" he asks.

Poised to take down the ten words, Katherine looks up.

"All right. Here are the ten words." Then Dr. Switzer stands up and yells, "Stop it or I'll bury you alive in a box!"

A terrified Katherine gathers her things and heads for the door.[4]

Do you think Jesus said, "Go and stop sinning" with the same tone Newhart used in this sketch? Is that how you picture God?

Many of us do. We read the 613 laws I mentioned, or other portions of Scripture, and picture a white-bearded God in the clouds, pointing his finger down at us whenever he catches us with our hands in the cookie jar.

But in the context of John 8, it seems that Christ has a different tone altogether. Jesus doesn't say, "Stop sinning, or I'll bury you alive in a box!" His tone sounds more like, "Stop sinning, or you'll find yourself in these kinds of situations again." Or, "Stop sinning, because you know this life leads nowhere."

The word translated "no more" means something closer to "no longer" or "not hereafter." Bible scholar Eugene Peterson may have rendered it best when he translated this as "From now on, don't sin" (MSG).

But those words of Jesus beg the question: How?

How do we stop sinning?

John didn't share with us whether Jesus continued a conversation with the woman caught and liberated. We are to assume she left with the benediction on her heart and a lot to think about. Did she return to living in sin? Did she resist for a season, then slide back into adultery months or years later? We half expect her to—because we struggle so much with this simple command: stop sinning.

DOWNLOADING SELF-CONTROL

I used to be able to sit down at a computer and type away for hours without distraction. Now there are instant messages, email inboxes, and, worst of all, social media sites to check. I find myself distracted. That's why I love an app I downloaded from the Internet that I can set to block social media and other sites for a given length of time. Believe it or not, I've used it to block even my ministry website. I can still do research or stream music, but Twitter, Facebook, and other distractions are locked out.

The app is called Self-Control. To get the app, I literally had to answer this question: "Do you want to download Self-Control?"

I thought, "Yes, Lord! Yes, I do!"

Don't you wish you could just download self-control for all areas of your life? Don't you wish it were as easy as a click of a button to stop eating, smoking, or looking at whatever know you shouldn't?

Of course you can't really download self-control. Instead we usually choose to "follow [our] arrow wherever it points," as Kasey Musgraves sings with a certain southern charm in her country song, telling us to "make lots of noise, kiss lots of boys, or kiss lots of girls, if that's something you're into."[5]

When trying to "just stop it" seems impossible, what do you do? Do you simply do what comes naturally, following whatever desires or urges drive you? What happens when kissing lots of boys leads to an unplanned pregnant or an STD? Musgraves goes on to sing about rolling up a joint to follow your arrow wherever it points. But what about when one too many joints gets you fined, flunked, or fired? Do you really want to live in a world where we all just follow our arrows? I bet you've already learned that this isn't a workable strategy for human life—especially when another person's arrow is pointing right at your head.

So where do we go from here? Musgraves feels caught in a no-win reality, so she sings, "You're damned if you do, and you're damned if you don't."

But Jesus said to the woman, "Neither do I condemn you" (John 8:11). He says you're not damned at all.

Jesus does two things: He forgives, and he empowers.

GO AND SIN NO MORE

We've seen others return to sin before, haven't we? We've seen it in ourselves too. But I think the woman caught in adultery did leave her life of sin. I think she went at the word *go*, and sinned no more.

If so, how?

First, she was truly at the end of her rope. There's nothing like brokenness to establish a turning point. There's nowhere to go but up when you're the guest of dishonor at a stoning. Have you reached your turning point? Have you been truly broken about your sin?

Second, the woman caught had a transforming encounter with the living God, who forgave her of her sin and didn't condemn her. Have you encountered that same God? Has Jesus made it clear that he knows your sin and that he could condemn you for it, but that he chooses not to? Look him in the face today and confirm this in your soul. Invite the presence of Jesus to transform the way you see sin in your life, and ask him to provide hope for change.

Third, this woman was empowered by the transforming power of forgiveness. She left Jesus, not with a Bob Newhart-style "Stop it" ringing in her ears, but with a full heart, thankful for her salvation, thankful for a second chance, and ready to not only leave her life of sin, but to live a life of joy.

Are you?

PRAYER

You are with me, Jesus. I have many accusers, and they may be right that I'm wrong, but I know you choose not to condemn me even though I deserve it. I confess that I have sinned. I'm guilty and deserve much less than you've offered me. But I am so grateful for the second chance. I owe you everything. Thank you, Jesus, my Redeemer!

FOR REFLECTION

1. Read John 8:1–11. Do you more often find yourself living in the role of the woman caught or the role of the Pharisees?

2. Why is it so hard for us to talk about sin without being either defensive of ourselves or judgmental of others? What is it about the presence of Jesus that helps us avoid either of those responses?

3. Do you think of your own sin and sinfulness often? What do you do about your sins? Informed by this passage, consider what you think Jesus might have you do differently.

4. Is it possible to do what Jesus told the woman to do? To stop sinning is difficult at best. How might that be possible for someone to do? Read these passages to inform your thinking: Hebrews 12:14; Philippians 4:8; Leviticus 20:7; Ephesians 1:4; 5:27; 1 Peter 1:15; 2:5; 2 Timothy 1:9; Colossians 1:22; Romans 12:1; 2 Corinthians 5:17; and Revelation 21:5.

9

MARGINALIZED

JOHN 9:1-34

My name is David, which means "beloved." I have been loved for sure. David was also a character in the Bible. I love to hear stories of David.

My boss's name is Jo Anne, which means "God is gracious." He has been gracious to her and through her. It is also a modern form of a biblical name; Joanna was one of the original disciples of Jesus.

Jo Anne has traveled to a part of India called Gujarat to meet with a doctor named Samuel. That name means "God hears." He has certainly heard us. Samuel is the prophet in the Bible who anointed David as king over Israel.

Samuel in Gujarat brought Jo Anne into a room where many children had been gathered. They were students in a new orphanage school. Samuel took Jo Anne aside and explained that most of those students were the children of prostitutes who were now dead. As he whispered into her ear, she looked out into the faces of the kids. He explained that because they had been born in that situation, they were the lowest of the low in the class-based Indian society—so low on the scale that no one had given them names.

Jo Anne looked out on their faces as the realization washed over her: Here was a crowd of school-age children who were so shamed and marginalized by society that they came to this orphanage with no identity.

People name pets; kids name stuffed animals. My family once had an aquarium, and we even named the fish. Imagine what it might be like to go through life without a name. Lower than a dog. Less important than a teddy bear. To leave someone unnamed is to treat them as if they do not exist.

To reach those on the margins of society is our task as Christians. Followers of Jesus Christ serve the last and least, not the fast and first.

We are called to love the lost and lonely, not the mighty with the most. While companies might target audiences with higher incomes and privilege in order to boost profits, the church of Christ starts with the shamed and maimed, the blamed and framed, the defamed and most certainly the unnamed marginalized like those children in Gujarat. Why is this so? Because the transforming presence of Jesus pulls those who are marginalized back to the center of our attention.

FROM BIRTH

Those who go blind lose what they have known, and that is precisely the loss. Having lost their sight, they can remember the look of a sunset, a mother's hands, or a lover's smile. But they can never see them again, and that is the regret.

Those who are blind from birth never know these things, and that is precisely the tragedy. They recall no sunsets, know a mother's hand by its texture alone, and if they have a lover, that love is truly blind. This is not to say that losing sight is better or worse than never having it—only different.

Jesus once came across a man who had never possessed sight. The "man born blind," as he has come to be known, didn't seek to speak with Jesus; rather, he was used as a prop for a theological question from the disciples: "Rabbi, who sinned, this man or his parents, that he was born blind?" (John 9:2).

There are no stupid questions, we are told. However, I do wonder if some questions might be inappropriately worded or timed. Some questions hurt. I was at a party where a friend went up to a woman he hadn't seen in some time, and, growing wide-eyed while looking at her midsection, asked, "When are you due?"

You guessed it—she wasn't pregnant. Perhaps there are stupid questions after all.

The question the disciples ask was loaded with assumptions we might consider stupid at face value. They see a man blind from birth, and in their minds there are only two options: either he had sinned or his parents had. Otherwise, they assumed, he wouldn't be in this condition.

OPTION A: HE SINNED

The man born blind was born on the wrong side of the good-and-evil tracks, and there was something about him that caused him to be cursed from birth. It was his fault. For those who like to assign blame, one option is to blame the man himself. This is the karma approach to the presence of suffering: bad things happen to bad people. So if bad things are happening to you, well, I hate to judge, but you can draw the conclusion for yourself.

OPTION B: HIS PARENTS SINNED

The parents must have done something wrong. They didn't read the right prenatal care books. Or they didn't pay their tithe while the wife was pregnant. They were bad, evil parents, and they were cursed with a blind child. This is the generational approach to suffering: bad things happen to bad families. So if bad things are happening to you, well, so sorry, but let's talk about how your mother messed up your life.

Hard to imagine making such silly assumptions, isn't it?

But wait. Don't we do this as well? Don't we frequently assign culpability when faced with a tragedy? We see people in bad situations and play like hall-of-fame blame gamers. When we see someone hit rock bottom, our response is more often "Serves them right" than "How can I serve them?" They did this to themselves, we reason. Or their parents did it. They are in a cycle of evil that is either their fault or the fault of their family. With a smug sense of our own success, we think, "Ain't it a shame that some people just don't get it?"

Jesus doesn't think that way. The disciples wanted to have a theological discussion about blame, but Jesus displayed a practical experience of God's glory. Jesus didn't take option A or option B. So he chose option C.

OPTION C: NEITHER SINNED

Jesus seems to have been saying, "Don't assume that all who hit rock bottom threw themselves there." He said the parents aren't to blame either. Jesus made it clear that assigning culpability is not our responsibility.

"'Neither this man nor his parents sinned,' said Jesus, 'but this happened so that the works of God might be displayed in him'" (v. 3).

The works of God were indeed displayed in him. Jesus healed the man born blind, right then and there. The diagnosis? A light case of blindness with an added opportunity for God to be glorified. The prescription? One part dirt, one part saliva. The outcome? Sight.

That sounds about right. That's the Jesus you and I know. Jesus makes miracles out of mud pies. A man who goes blind loses what he knows, and that is precisely the loss. A man who is blind from birth never knew sight, and that is precisely the tragedy. A man who was blind from birth but now can see? That is precisely the work of God displayed in him.

Let's be option C people. When we find the marginalized, whom everyone assumes got themselves into the mess they're in, let's choose to see them as human beings God wants his works to be displayed in. Then perhaps God will display his works through us as well. Option C people know that displaying God's glory, not the assignment of blame, is the goal.

God had been glorified already in Samuel's life, the doctor in Gujarat, India. Samuel was born nearly as marginalized as the nameless kids in his orphanage. He was born blind. His mother had converted to Christianity, so they were thrown out of their village. This modern-day Man Born Blind lived on the outskirts of society and was about as marginalized as they come.

But Samuel's mother had ideas. She was an option C person. She felt strongly that God had a purpose for Samuel's life that didn't match his blindness. She took her boy aside and placed her hands on his face, covering his eyes. She prayed that God would heal him so he could do what God had planned for him. Samuel received his sight. God always sees the option C. God still makes miracles out of mud pies.

GUILT AND SHAME

Guilt is good. Shame is bad.

God uses guilt to change us. When we have done something wrong, our guilt sensors go off. In fact, we wouldn't even know we had done something wrong unless we experienced good guilt. Our conscience is an internal instrument that can be used before we do something contrary to the will of God, or afterward. So a guilty conscience is a helpful thing. People who say that they have no regrets surely do not mean it. To have no regrets is to have no conscience — or to be an absolutely perfect person. Only some kind of monster would be the former, and only Christ could claim to be the latter.

We all live with regret. What we regret is sin. We take our regret over sin to God and he forgives us. The blood of Christ redeems our sin and our guilt goes away. When we regret something, we are saying we would do it differently if we could do it over again. We "get convicted about it." Even after receiving forgiveness, we have a "conviction" about things like that. This is what it means to be redeemed; guilt can be a good thing when used by God.

However, shame is not useful for change. Brené Brown says, "Shame corrodes the very part of us that believes we can change and do better."[1] Guilt motivates us to seek God for forgiveness, and that's good. Shame may motivate, but only unsustainably. Shame produces perpetual motivation to please others in order to alleviate shame in a short-term way. Who can please all people all the time? There is no end to the pleasing of others. Too often those who are shamed run into the arms of their abusers—an endless cycle of chasing the wind.

Pleasing others cannot alleviate guilt. Guilt is a matter of law. A judge who has proper authority is the only one who can judge you guilty. When you are guilty, you take your punishment, and serve your sentence. If you've done the crime, you do the time. You pay the price for your guilt. But notoriously when it comes to shame, others cannot alleviate it for the simple reason that shame causes you to hide from relationships.

Guilt is a feeling, whereas shame is a state, like a room or a place. One feels guilty, but one is "in" shame, perhaps even dying in it. You eat the forbidden fruit, and that is wrong, so you *feel* guilt. But it is the running to hide, as Adam and Eve did, and the act of covering up the naked sin—that is the *state* of shame. Guilt is when our God-given conscience alerts us to wrongdoing. God gives us guilt for a positive function. But shame is what happens when we run from it, cover it up, or distract others from it.

Shame is a cancerous overgrowth of sin. The one in a state of shame might not even feel much about it—good or bad. Shame is what Carl

Jung called a soul-eating emotion. It is the ultimate demotivator. Shame is a disease that wastes away the person. Whereas guilt seeks forgiveness and reconciliation, shame runs from both. Where guilt may push us, shame paralyzes us. "Shame is like melting. You can actually feel your muscles sag and drop, as if your body is preparing you to crawl, or possibly ooze, to the nearest exit," says Maureen Johnson.[2]

We learned what to do about guilt in chapter 8; now let's talk about what to do about shame.

HAVE YOU BEEN WITH JESUS?

The only solution for shame is to reach out and heal the relationship, which you cannot do while holding the sword of shame in your hand. That is why grasping relationship requires letting shame go. Shame is a sword with no handle; you cannot hold on to it without being cut. The great benefit of wanting to be rid of shame is that you are the only one who can rid yourself of the self-destructive sword in the first place—so that desire is the place to start.

Your family can't release your grip from shame. No amount of encouragement from spouse, parents, siblings, or children can wrest the sword from you. You may be in shame for the way you have treated them or they have treated you, but they can't release you. Only you can let the shame sword go so you can reach out to them.

A counselor or a pastor can't release you from shame. In fact, you won't even truly deeply discuss your shame with a counselor until you start to let it go. Talking with that counselor or pastor while walking away from the shame sword can keep you from picking it up again, but a counselor or pastor can't release it for you. You must let it go.

Even God will not release you from your shame unless you cease picking it up again. He gave you guilt as a good gift. But he did not give you shame. He can tell you that he loves you, he can offer you forgiveness for guilt—but in order for you to be in right relationship with God, you must decide yourself to let your shame go and seek freedom in the grace of Jesus Christ.

The shame sword is in your hand. Will you lay it down and seek healing? If you lay down the sword, the wounds may still be there, in fact they will be, but you have taken the first step to facing the sun. If you start walking in that direction, the shadows of shame will always be behind you.

Most families have a favorite sport. It might be soccer, hockey, swimming, baseball, or even cricket. When I was growing up, my family's favorite sport was arguing. Some families watched football on Sunday afternoon. We watched a political talk show called *The McLaughlin Group*. Pundits and analysts of all political persuasions argued the topics of the day. Our family affectionately called it *The Arguing Show*.

At the dinner table, we would reenact our own version of *The Arguing Show* most nights. We debated all kinds of issues, even confronting each other about our behavior. Most other people might have considered this bizarre and unhealthy, but for us it was just normal. We still do it today. A few years ago, while on a family vacation, my brother and I had a five-hour argument about the Bible with my dad (he says he won the argument, but we claim that's only because he retreated from his original position).

When my brother was a young teenager, we had one of our epic family arguments at the dinner table. I was an older teenager, nearly ready to move out of the house. My parents were trying to convince my brother to do something differently, because his behavior was hurting his reputation a bit with his peers. I wasn't deeply involved in the argument. My brother was holding his own arguing with our parents. In fact, they weren't changing his mind at all. So I inserted myself, acting like the older, wiser veteran teenager. As I got involved, my parents were glad to see that I might be siding with them—until they heard my advice. I said, "When you're a teenager, all that matters is what other people think about you."

It think it took my parents awhile to walk that one back. Not exactly the advice they were looking for.

The world teaches us the bad advice I gave my brother, doesn't it? The unspoken rule is this: All that matters is what people think of you.

So when others shame us, when we are marginalized by a culture of shame, Jesus walks up to us and says, "You may have been born blind, but you can live free if you release your shame and grasp me."

SHAMING THE SINNER

The Pharisees were a part of a shaming culture, which they had helped create. In John 9:28, when the man born blind asked the Pharisees if they wanted to become disciples of Jesus, "they hurled insults at him." In verse 34, they showed all their cards as option B people and said, "You were steeped in sin at birth; how dare you lecture us!"

We religious types tend to do this, don't we? We feel that others are insulting us or questioning our beliefs merely by living differently than we do. The fact that others conduct themselves differently shouldn't surprise us. If we believe our own doctrines, we should expect that those who do not share them *will* live differently. Yet we respond to this perceived challenge with shame language. When we use shame as our primary tool to communicate truth, we are no different from the

Pharisees of John 9. Shame is a double-edged sword with no handle. When you wield it against others, everyone gets cut.

Too often we think that sharing the gospel means dominating a debate. We make every conversation about faith a competition with winners and losers, which merely causes others to avoid us. This tactic betrays the fact that most of us are not as smart as we think we are.

I have been able to defeat others in debate merely because I was more eloquent than they were, but that doesn't mean they were wrong and I was right. It just means I can argue better. Debating is an acquired skill, one I honed for many years on the family *Arguing Show*. Jesus, however, did not call us to be skilled debaters but to be bearers of grace.

Even when religious debates do yield a victor, the exercise is merely intellectual at its core and does not produce heart change. In that sense, debate is not really faith sharing but instead an intellectual shaming of the other. Shaming the sinner is not the same thing as sharing the gospel. How have we confused this point?

Shaming the sinner is about anger; sharing the gospel is about joy. Your faith should make you more content and at peace in sharing truth with those far from God, not angry with them.

Shaming the sinner is based on competitiveness, but sharing the gospel is about a love story. No one can argue with your faith journey, but competitiveness ignites defensiveness.

Shaming the sinner is rightly perceived as judgmentalism, but sharing the gospel brings hope. Faith makes us hope for a better future for others, not a painful punishment.

Shaming the sinner becomes frustrating, but sharing the gospel results in love. Our faith produces unconditional motivation to freely share, not frustration at those who think or act differently than we do.

Shaming the sinner focuses on the past, but sharing the gospel is about the future. It anticipates the best-case scenario and asks, "What could result if they did follow Christ?"

Shaming the sinner is a fruitless way of doing evangelism. It goes nowhere. Instead of shaming the sinner, we can share the gospel with honesty, grace, and compassion with those who are not yet in relationship with God.

NEW NAMES

Shaming others is not sharing the gospel. So if someone has shamed and marginalized you, don't hold on to that. They're wrong. What they say about you is not your identity in Christ. In Jesus you can say, "I have been crucified with Christ and I no longer live, but Christ lives in me" (Gal. 2:20). You can claim that "though they stumble, they will never fall, for the LORD holds them by the hand" (Ps. 37:24 NLT).

Others may try to move you to the margins, but wherever Jesus is you will find yourself in the middle of everything that matters. Don't let shame overcome you because "anyone who believes in him will never be put to shame" (Rom. 10:11).

A man named Red was well-known in our town because he walked the streets as a salesman of sorts: He himself was for sale. A mutual friend sent me texts describing the spiritual conversations she was having with Red, a male prostitute, and that she had invited him to our church. He said, "There's no way someone like me could show up at church." She asked me via text: "So, pastor, is it OK, or not?"

I started dialing right away: "Of course Red can come to church. In fact, I'm back in town tomorrow, and, if he would be willing, I'd like the three of us to meet." She brought Red to the church office that Wednesday at noon. Red was a 120-pound young man with hair dyed orange who wore sunglasses even though we were inside.

Our long conversation started with the backstory. I found out Red's real name. We spent time a good deal of time talking about identity, sexuality, and the struggle with sin. We told him that we loved him and would help him. Then we spent even more time talking about God and salvation. We walked through several passages in the book of Romans together, using the Bible we'd just given him, the first he'd ever owned. Then we walked the aisle together, kneeling for his one-on-one altar call with Jesus Christ. He gave his life to Jesus right there, and then he wrote his name—his real name—in the front of his Bible, along with the date, only moments after God wrote his name in the Book of Life.

This young man had experienced only shame from Christians and the church. He had no hope for his soul, no hope that he would ever be loved, accepted, and included in the church. He thought it was policy to exclude "his kind." However, we looked up God's policy and found that beautiful word *whosoever* in John 3:16 (KJV). Whoever, from wherever, having done whatever, are all caught up in that beautiful word *whosoever*. Despite his past, he fit the "whosoever" clause of Christ, who so loved the world—all of it.

Many think there is no hope for him. Many communicated that to him in the past. Some still do. To him, church had been a place of holiness, a place you could go only if you had your act already together. It was a club for the already complete, not those under construction, a place for holy people who offered no hope, a place of shame where he would only be marginalized. So he never went, never even thought he was allowed to. But in Jesus, he found true hope, and a church that found its holiness only in Christ in the first place.

I WAS . . . NOW I . . .

What new name has God given you? What did God save you from, or where would you be if you didn't have Christ in you? The man born blind stood before the religious authorities and said, "One thing I do know. I was blind but now I see!" (John 9:25). That's the best testimony he could have given. That's hard to argue with. How would you say something similar about your life?

I asked a group of Christians to describe what God has done for them, and here are some of their answers:

- I was a thief, now I give.
- I was physically broken, now I'm healed.
- I was wasting away, now I'm fulfilled.
- I was unforgiving, now I forgive.
- I was confused, now I have purpose.
- I was critical, now I'm understanding.
- I was arrogant, now I'm humbled.
- I was rejected and sad, now I'm accepted and joyful.
- I was insecure, now I have an identity.
- I was afraid, now I'm bold.
- I was lonely, now I'm loved.
- I was inadequate, now I have worth.
- I was running away, now I'm home.
- I was religious, now I'm saved.
- I was a worrier, now I trust in God.
- I was fearful, now I'm peaceful.
- I was addicted, now I'm free.
- I was broken and depressed, now I have joy.

- I was self-driven, now I'm Spirit-directed.
- I was ashamed, now I'm proud.
- I was tricked into sin, now I'm forgiven and free.
- I was passing the buck, now I take responsibility.
- I was in the dark, now I'm in the light.
- I was empty, now I'm being filled.
- I was bound, now I'm free.

Do any of those describe your story? If so, circle it. If not, fill in these blanks:

I was _____,

now I _____.

Samuel didn't let those orphans in Gujarat, India, go on without a name. The people at the orphanage named each child. They gave them names from Scripture, names like Ruth, which means "friend," or Peter, which means "rock," or Sarah, which means "Princess." They would give a boy a name like Matthew, which means "gift of God," and then tell him the story of Matthew, saying, "That's your story now; that's your name." They would give a girl a name like Elizabeth, which means "the fullness of God," and then tell her that story.

In the kingdom of God, nobody is marginalized. Jesus frees the marginalized from the shame our culture puts on people. No one goes without a name once Jesus shows up. The transforming presence of Jesus pulls those who are marginalized back to the center of our attention, even giving them honor.

In Christ you can leave shame behind and find a solution for your sin. People may move you to the margins, but just move closer to Christ.

Wherever you encounter Jesus, you'll find yourself in the middle of everything that matters. More often than not, that's on the margins anyway.

PRAYER

You are with me, Jesus. I have felt left out so often, Lord, and it's so good to know that I can find you on the margins. Thank you for releasing me from my shame and providing for my physical and emotional healing. Help me to find others who are marginalized and to help them know they always have a name and place with you. Thank you, Jesus, my encourager!

FOR REFLECTION

1. What does your name mean? What do you like about it? What don't you like? If you were to get a new name from God, what would you hope it would be or mean?

2. Read John 9:1–34. Where do you see shame in the passage?

3. Has anyone been a source of shame in your life? Is there anyone who tries to shame you even now? Do you put shame on yourself? How can you let go of this sword with no handle?

4. What words did you put into the blanks above?

10

GRIEVED

JOHN 11:1–44

n 1813 J. J. Audubon rode his horse to Louisville from his house in Henderson, Kentucky. On his way, the author of the legendary book *The Birds of America* saw a great black mass traveling toward him in the sky. The ever-dutiful naturalist pulled out his journal to record, "The light of noon-day was obscured as by an eclipse." The darkened sky was not from an eclipse or some doomsday catastrophe. It was birds. Just birds, blotting out the sun with their immense congregation.

Pigeons form a spectacle that stunned the bird biographer. "The air was literally filled with pigeons," Audubon wrote in his journal. And not just any pigeons; these were the passenger pigeons of North America. They flock together in amazingly large groups. He paused for three days to watch the mass migration. Audubon pulled out his slide-rule while watching the amazing number of pigeons cover the shores of the Ohio River for miles and miles before moving on. He estimated that this one flock alone had 1,115,136,000 pigeons in it (around 1.1 billion).[1]

THE LAST PASSENGER

Plato said that birds of a feather flock together, and no bird proved the saying more than the passenger pigeon. Their largest documented nesting occurred in 1871 in Wisconsin: "An estimated 136 million breeding birds covered some 850 square miles of forest." Another flock flew over Ontario in 1860 and was estimated to number three times the size of the one Audubon saw. Yes, that's 3.7 *billion* birds.[2]

But it was not to be so forever. Firearms enabled mass hunting of passenger pigeons, and in just forty years their numbers decreased from the billions to the hundreds of thousands, and by the turn of the century they were nearly extinct.

Extinction is usually noticed only after the fact. We look around and realize that a species has disappeared. Then we analyze what happened. But with passenger pigeons, we know the exact year, month, day, and hour of extinction. And we even know the name of the last pigeons. Her name was Martha.

Martha and her male pigeon partner had lived their entire lives in the Cincinnati Zoo. Outlasting a few dozen of their captive counterparts, Martha saw her mate die, and as so often happens after an individual loses a loved one, she then began to brood and decline, seemingly aware that her passing meant the loss of not only her life but of her kind.

Martha died at 1:00 p.m. Eastern Time on September 1, 1914. Solemn zookeepers boxed Martha's remains in ice and sent her off to the Smithsonian, where she continues to be on display. Once numbering in the billions, Martha's remains are all that is left of the passenger pigeon. Gone.

Nineteen hundred or so years before pigeon Martha's death, another Martha mourned a different death—that of her dear brother, Lazarus. Lazarus, Martha, and their sister Mary were the closest friends Jesus seems to have had on earth. We don't know why. We know only that they lived near Jerusalem, and they were devoted to the teachings of Jesus. We know he stayed with them from time to time. Martha cooked him meals and pampered him on his visits. Mary poured perfume over Jesus' feet at a feast and listened to his stories (see John 12). Lazarus stayed up late into the night praying with him, and the three shared many a meal laughing with him. These three were like siblings for the Savior, a second family for the Son of Man.

By the eleventh chapter of the book of John, Jesus and his disciples had fled the area around Jerusalem because of a plot to kill him. While up north in Galilee, word came to Jesus that his friend Lazarus was sick. Rather than take off south immediately, he waited a few days. Then, sensing his friend had died from the illness, he traveled south with a heavy heart. The presence of Jesus is possible even in the midst of heart-rending grief; in fact perhaps it is most probable there, as he's been there himself.

HAVE YOU BEEN WITH JESUS?

Have you known such grief? Has your heart ached for no biological reason but for the loss of a loved one? Have you been here? I recall my coworker Candace, who lost her marriage and shortly thereafter lost her mother, who was her best friend. I think of dozens of wives I know who have lost husbands to heart attacks. I think of dozens of husbands I know who have lost wives to cancer. I think of Dina, who lost her parents in a plane crash when she was just a child. I think of Mary Beth, whose husband was killed in a car crash. There are so many stunning losses one may experience, whether in slow motion, like the gradual deterioration of leukemia, or suddenly, as with the violent crashing of a car. Death crashes our world.

I think of my friend Karen, whose husband, Ross, died in a freak excavation accident in their backyard. I mentioned Ross in chapter 2. I remember, eleven months after his death, meeting Karen on a flight of stairs and stopping to chat. They say that coping with loss is supposed to get easier over time, but she talked of not being able to sleep or eat, and I realized that her pain had not subsided one bit in nearly a year. I had traveled to Africa with Ross, who was a humanitarian, fund-raiser, and business owner. I looked up to him a great deal. He might have been the most holy, humble, and hardworking man I've ever known. But he was taken for no good reason at all. I, too, still grieve this loss more than a year later. It makes me just a little mad, to be truthful. It just makes no sense.

In these moments, we realize how much presence matters. I was recently with a group of twenty of my friends, and we began sharing about major losses in our lives. One by one we recounted how someone showed up in the darkest moments, just to be with us. One woman shared about losing her husband after a horrible fifteen-year sickness. Some college students, who didn't even know them, showed up to be with them in the final hours. Two of my buddies shared about losing their dads when they were young, and how each had close pals who canceled everything to travel to be with them through it. Another shared of nearly dying of cancer himself and being wracked with pain and doubt. His pastor spent countless hours just being with him. Though the pastor said little, just him being there meant everything. My friend broke down crying as he shared how much it meant to him. This kind of presence is a flicker of light amid the dark shadow of death. In these moments we imitate the transforming presence of Jesus most clearly: "The light shines in the darkness, and the darkness has not overcome it" (John 1:5).

Sometimes just being present doesn't seem to be enough. I remember Sarah, the mother of Carter, and Brittani, the mother of Elijah. These mothers each gave birth to sons who died within hours. I think of them cradling those lifeless limbs, those tiny newborn bodies awash in tears. In such situations, a greeting card line cannot bridge the painful chasm any more than I could leap across the Grand Canyon. If you've ever attended a funeral where a tiny casket was displayed at the front of the chapel, you know that death doesn't always make sense. Maybe it never does.

It didn't make sense for me when I was twelve years old. My first traumatic encounter with death came with the passing of my uncle Elmer, my father's only sibling. My dad was born ten years after Elmer and, as a child, couldn't pronounce his name. So he called him Memo. This nickname stuck, and the family called him that for years. Uncle Memo died of a massive heart attack at the age of fifty. A man who had given his entire career to the kingdom of God, helping train ministers of the gospel, raising funds for Christian schools, and pastoring churches was gone in a moment. He died in his bedroom with his teenage son, my cousin, fruitlessly trying to revive him.

I remember standing near the casket at the funeral home. The receiving line stretched around the block, as it sometimes does for too-soon deaths like these. My aunt wailed uncontrollably, sitting limply on the couch, not so much hugged as upheld from the floor by her friends. My grandfather, the gentlest soul those who met him ever knew, scooted up to the casket in his wheelchair. He reached out his hand and patted the hands of the dead. He said, calmly, "You were a good boy."

We all grieved deeply. My grandpa grieved for only six months, however. He died of a broken heart, some of us say; the doctors called it another heart attack. I grieve that too-soon loss to this day as well.

Grief does not end as soon as people say it does. Arbitrary time-lines measured by calendars seem so superficial in the face of such loss. My son is a close pal to four of Uncle Memo's grandsons, who never knew their grandfather. When I think about that, as I am now, I tear up all over again, nearly thirty years after he died.

I'm not alone. My uncle's best friend, Earle, became one of the leaders of our denomination and one of the most known and powerful preachers among our people. He is anything but the fragile, sensitive type. However, years after my uncle Memo's death, he confessed to my father that sometimes he would be driving alone in a car on some highway in the middle of nowhere and begin thinking of his friend Elmer. Earle would find himself, an hour later, with a face full of tears, still grieving a long-lost friend.

What are we to do with all this grief?

MAD, SAD, GLAD

The first thing we must do when facing grief is admit the sadness. Perhaps this is easy for you, but many of us don't admit we are grieving or do not take the time to actually grieve for fear it will bring out emotions we cannot face.

I've had to learn to keep a closer eye on what I grieve, even the simple things like a failure or a lost friendship over conflict. It's a part of a larger process I want to share with you.

I learned this while hearing Pete Scazzero teach at a pastors' event in Michigan (Scazzero is the author of *Emotionally Healthy Spirituality*). He shared a simple rubric for processing how we feel, thus sorting out our emotions. The rubric is called "Sad, Mad, and Glad." When I am having time alone with God, either an extended time away or just a few moments in the car, I find that I use this to pause and sort things out.

I AM MAD

I usually have to start with being mad. I build a list of those who are ticking me off. I think through the kinds of things that are making me angry during this time. I review in my head the comments on social media that have made me mad. I think about situations that make me mad. I just have a grand ol' angry time with a lot of gnashing of teeth.

You might think this is a bit odd and that I shouldn't embrace such angry times of prayer (although I'd point you to the Psalms to defend myself; they tend to get pretty angry at times).[3] I do find that these angry feelings are in me whether I admit them or not, and when I do not admit them and work through them, they end up motivating my actions later in ways that are unhealthy, overbearing, or over-correcting. As Joseph Grenny says, "If you don't talk it out, you'll act it out."[4] However, when all is said and done, I find that some of the things I feel mad about I am actually just *sad* about.

I AM SAD

My default reaction is to be mad about things that are unjust or tragic, but that doesn't allow for the appropriate grief. In part, I should just be sad about the things I'm initially angry about. I find that when I am mad about something, I don't get over it. Perhaps that's OK for some things that I should be perpetually working on. Other things, however, I really do need to heal over. This is especially true when it comes to the things I am personally impacted by. I should be sad about them, not just mad.

I make this distinction by reserving my righteous anger for broader injustices rather than things that hurt only me. It also helps me sort out what things really don't hurt me directly, and where I'm overcompensating by carrying the grievance of another when that is not really my right or duty. I might not have all the information needed to truly carry that grievance with accuracy or with an appropriately open door for reconciliation. As a pastor, I've found that some people may carry a grudge about something done to someone close to them long after the person actually harmed has forgiven the offender and been reconciled through the grace of Christ. When I feel the grievance of another more deeply than they do, I have to check my motives.

When I get to this sad part of my internal processing, I tend to cry about things I didn't realize I was sensitive about. I cry about friendships that I seem to be losing, dreams that are dying, leaders who are disappointing, or even projects that seem to have failed. I don't cry about these things around other people; in fact I tend to act a little edgy about them with other people, which is why I need this grieving process. But when just God and I are talking about them, he helps me see that I'm just plain old sad. And that's OK.

Sometimes we just need to say, "I am sad." We need a good cry, an appropriate grieving. Some things have been lost that were gained. Dreams have not been realized. Friends have died. Family members are dying or have died. We grieve. That is right and good.

I AM GLAD

After I clarify the things I'm mad and sad about, I feel convicted by God to think about the things I'm truly glad about. After grieving friendships I seem to be losing, I celebrate new friends I'm making. After admitting some dreams are dying, I dream up some new ones that are even better. After shaking my head at some leaders who are disappointing to me, I remind myself of the hundreds more who inspire me with their courage and integrity.

After listing the names of those who have died, I list those who have been born. Sometimes that includes literal babies. I celebrate the new little ones. Sometimes I am thinking of those who have come to Christ and found new birth and life in him—sometimes through the testimony of the dearly departed.

Then I am able to see the forest for the trees and start to name the treasures of my life that give me joy, starting with my salvation, my family, and my church.

At these times, I can truly receive some gifts of gladness from God and move past cynicism and skepticism to enjoy life again, and even smile when remembering lost loved ones.

Those are the ways I cope. Perhaps it will help you. But don't take them as rules, just ideas that may be of help. Remember that when it came to grief, Jesus broke all the rules, especially at the funeral of Lazarus.

BREAKING THE FUNERAL RULES

Jesus arrived in Bethany, near Jerusalem, and his actions made for a great list of things not to do at a funeral.

The first thing you don't do at a funeral is tell people to open the casket if it is closed. If it's closed, it's closed for a reason. Who are you to ask the family to open it? This is a major no-no. But he broke this rule.

"Jesus, once more deeply moved, came to the tomb. It was a cave with a stone laid across the entrance. 'Take away the stone,' he said" (John 11:38–39). Ever the conscientious one, Martha resisted, saying it had been four days since Lazarus was buried, so the odor of the body would be very strong. But Jesus broke this rule, and they opened the tomb.

The second thing you don't do at a funeral is make wild claims. You're not supposed to make big, bold, declarative statements. In Pastoral Counseling 101, I learned to say things like, "I'm so sorry for your loss" or "He is in a better place." I learned that the number one rule of funeral-going is to avoid attracting attention. Just show up; be there. Jesus broke this rule.

He told Martha, "The one who believes in me will live, even though they die; and whoever lives by believing in me will never die" (vv. 25–26). This is preposterous-sounding stuff. There he was at a funeral, saying that people don't die if they believe. Did he mean that Lazarus didn't believe? Was he deluding himself into thinking Lazarus wasn't really dead? Had Jesus lost touch with reality in his grief? You don't make wild claims at a funeral, but Jesus did.

The third rule of funerals is this: Don't talk to the dead. You talk to the family. You talk to the other mourners. You have hallway reunions with old friends and say things like, "So sorry we have to reunite under these circumstances, but it's good to see you." You don't ever speak to the dead. That's crazy talk. Not even the preacher directs comments to the casket. The sermon is not for the dead; it's for the living.

Not for Jesus. He broke this rule too, the biggest one of all. As if he were completely off his rocker, Jesus didn't deliver a sermon to the family, the crowd of mourners, or those there to see what was going to happen next. Nope. Jesus spoke to the dead.

If I did this, I would be ushered out the door or taken by the pastors to an office far from the sanctuary. But when Jesus speaks to the dead, they listen. What we learn from Lazarus is that when Jesus does an altar call at a funeral, even the corpse comes forward. Jesus performed a resurrection. Lazarus, his friend, had died. He was just a body. Cold. Lifeless. Until Jesus spoke. How did this happen? Who is this man, this man who raises the dead?

John told us at least seven things about Jesus.

1. Jesus *loves*. This man, Jesus, is the kind of man who loves people — that's because he is God in the flesh, and God defines love. When Mary and Martha sent the first-century version of a telegram to Jesus

in verse 3, it read, "Lord, the one you love is sick." Verse 5 confirms it: "Jesus loved Martha and her sister and Lazarus."

So Jesus, God the Son, of course developed relationships of love and companionship with people in his proximity just as we do. He is fully God and was also fully human. Whatever else you might know about him, remind yourself constantly that Jesus loves because God loves.

2. Jesus *knows*. He is unlike us in that he knows what we don't know. "After he had said this, he went on to tell them, 'Our friend Lazarus has fallen asleep; but I am going there to wake him up'" (v. 11). No telegram or smoke signal tipped him off to this. Mary didn't text Jesus, saying, "JC: the 1 u ♥ = dead." He just *knew*. Spend much time with the Son of Man in Scripture and you'll be certain Jesus knew things he wasn't supposed to know.

3. Jesus *risks*. The disciples and Jesus had just left the area around Jerusalem because it was dangerous. But Jesus said they were going to return: "Let us go back to Judea." The disciples protested. "'But Rabbi,' they said, 'a short while ago the Jews there tried to stone you, and yet you are going back?'" (vv. 7–8).

Jesus was willing to risk it. He not only loves, he knows what we don't know, and so he is willing to risk what we would not risk. The disciples go along with the fatalistic support of their ever-faithful doubting brother, Thomas, who "said to the rest of the disciples, 'Let us also go, that we may die with him'" (v. 16). Jesus risks in ways we would not risk because he knows something we don't know.

4. Jesus *speaks*. When Jesus arrived, he spoke truth to the situation. It reminds me that a funeral is not merely a time for grieving. A funeral is a time for truth telling. Jesus spoke the truth at this funeral. He shed tears, while also sharing truth. And he did so "plainly" (v. 14).

5. Jesus *claims*. This Jesus is not merely a man, which is why he knows what he knows, speaks what he speaks, and risks what he risks. He said it plainly to Martha: "I am the resurrection and the life" (v. 25). For Martha, and other Jews who believed in the resurrection, the concept was an event. It was a moment in time somewhere in the distant future—not in her lifetime for sure. To Martha, the resurrection was a post-apocalyptic fantasy that she partly believed in but that didn't have much relevance for her when grieving over her brother. Lazarus would rise in the "last day" she said (v. 24), implying "not today."

Jesus contradicted that. He said that he himself is the embodiment of the resurrection that is to come. He is the living, breathing, walking, talking, one-man apocalypse show. And his best buddy was not going to die on his watch. Jesus is the Son of God, and so he claimed what no one else can claim.

6. Jesus *weeps*. This verse is much more than a favorite verse for children to memorize at my church in order to get a treat from Pastor Judy (The hardest part is remembering the reference!)

In this verse, we see that even though Jesus knows what we don't know, risks what we wouldn't risk, and speaks what we would not speak, making claims we cannot claim, he is still like us. Because he loves personally, it leads him to weep in spite of all he knows, risks, speaks, and claims.

The Jews noticed that the Prophet was weeping at the loss of a friend, and they said, "See how he loved him!" (v. 36). Jesus cried at funerals. Doesn't that mean a whole lot to you? It does to me. This was not just a one-off tear on the cheek, given for show. As Mary approached Jesus, falling at his feet yet again, Jesus was moved. "When Jesus saw her weeping, and the Jews who had come along with her also weeping, he was deeply moved in spirit and troubled"

(v. 33). The word translated here as "deeply moved in spirit" is actually the word for "groan." Have you been there? Have you found yourself in a spot where you could only groan, "Oh, no"? Jesus did.

Let's take a moment to sidetrack on the fact that Jesus weeps. To do so, let's look at the funeral of one of the kings of England.

That England's king Edward VII (1841–1910) lived to the age of sixty-eight is astonishing in and of itself. Known as a voracious eater who smoked a dozen cigars and even more cigarettes every day, the king could not climb a flight of stairs without pausing to catch his breath.[5]

But he lived to what was a fairly advanced age for the time in which he died. When a monarch passes, the whole country goes into mourning. About six days after Edward's death, the canon at St. Paul's Cathedral, a man named Henry Scott Holland, felt he should address the topic of death in his sermon "The King of Terrors."

I've heard some bad funeral sermons in my time. I've even preached a few, I suppose. But no sermon on death, in my opinion, is worse than Henry Scott Holland's. Here are a few lines: "Death is nothing at all. It does not count. I have only slipped away into the next room. Nothing has happened. Everything remains exactly as it was. I am I, and you are you, and the old life we lived so fondly together is untouched."

He said later in the sermon, "It is not death; nobody is dead. It would be too ludicrous to suppose it. What has death to do with us? How can we die? Everything that we cared for and loved exists. Physical death has no meaning, no relation to it."[6]

Nearly every phrase of these lines is wrong. Death is very much something and certainly is not nothing. Something has indeed happened at death. Our deceased loved ones are not in the next room. They are in the next life. Our lives are not untouched by the deaths;

they are deeply touched. Things aren't exactly as they were, and we are deeply changed by death.

One only needs to look at the author of life and the defeater of death, Jesus Christ, to know this truth. He is deeply touched. While he knows that death can be beaten, that knowledge does not lessen his grief. He weeps. He groans. He's troubled. Physical death had meaning, very deep meaning, in that moment for Jesus, the one who would shortly thereafter die for us. His death was not nothing either. It was something. You might say it was everything.

To be a follower of Jesus is not to be chipper at funerals, to laugh off death, to scoff at the grim reaper. To be a follower of Jesus is to weep as he wept.

7. Jesus *raises*. He knows what we don't know and claims things we couldn't claim, while speaking what we wouldn't speak and risking what we wouldn't risk. Despite all this, he loves so deeply that he weeps as we would weep. Because of all this, because of who he is, Jesus raised Lazarus from the dead: "So they took away the stone. Then Jesus looked up and said, 'Father, I thank you that you have heard me. I knew that you always hear me, but I said this for the benefit of the people standing here, that they may believe that you sent me.' When he had said this, Jesus called in a loud voice, 'Lazarus, come out!' The dead man came out, his hands and feet wrapped with strips of linen, and a cloth around his face.' Jesus said to them, 'Take off the grave clothes and let him go'" (John 11:41–44).

Death isn't as final as we think. Jesus said as much all the way back in verse 4 of this chapter: "This sickness will not end in death. No, it is for God's glory so that God's Son may be glorified through it." And so Jesus raised his friend from the dead. A wonderful resurrection meant to foreshadow another to come, which would have even more significance than this one because it carried the weight of the sin of all humanity. Jesus not only raised Lazarus from the dead, he raised himself. He beat death, and resurrection came for us all in his power.

This is why the presence of Jesus is possible even in the midst of heart-rending grief; in fact perhaps it is most probable there, as he's been there himself, and conquered death himself.

THE LAST PASSENGERS

Earlier I shared about Martha. Not the sister of Lazarus, I mean the bird. Martha was the last passenger pigeon, now peacefully at rest, stuffed, literally, in the Smithsonian.

A group of part-scientists, part-activists, part-philosophers, led by Stewart Brand, are interested in a new field known as resurrection biology. Brand and his colleagues want to bring the passengers back in an effort they call revive and restore.[7] They would like to use genetic material from Martha the pigeon to recreate the passenger pigeon through biological experimentation. I know what you're thinking. The *Jurassic Pigeons* script must already be in development.

Guy Raz interviewed Dr. Brand for TED Radio and referred to the plan for de-extinction as "Stewart Brand's plan for hacking into the animal kingdom and bringing Martha back."[8] That struck me as untrue. No matter how advanced the science becomes, even if they have amazing success and bring out of that genetic material a new, or should I say, old species, it will not be a resurrection. He may be gifted, brilliant even, but Dr. Brand can't bring Martha back. Only God can pull off a true resurrection.

Jesus didn't need to hack the genome, because he wove the genome in the first place. He didn't need a lab. He just needed them to move the stone away. Jesus didn't find some similar species and "resurrect" Lazarus by growing him in a test tube. He brought the real Lazarus back from the dead. And he can resurrect the Lazarus you know and grieve. He'll resurrect you too, in his time.

I'd love to see a passenger pigeon in a zoo someday, regrown for visitation by Stewart Brand and his group of biological hackers. I'd like to stroll up to the de-extinction aviary, a more peaceful vision of Jurassic Park. I'd like to hear their song, which has been silent for more than a hundred years.

But one day a much greater feat will be accomplished. It will be a greater task than reviving and restoring birds. It will be a more consequential phenomenon than de-extinction. Our righteous and resurrected Savior, with tears still in his eyes, will in turn resurrect us. He will revive our spirits and restore all things, and he will begin by literally and specifically resurrecting our bodies. Your body. My body. All bodies.[9] There will be no last human passengers on planet Earth. For all eternity, the resurrected will worship the Son in the restored heaven and earth.

Billions of us will walk up to him on resurrected limbs. That's right, billions with a *b*. All of us will be able to embrace him with resurrected arms. We will talk to him with resurrected tongues and touch his resurrected hands with our own resurrected hands. "Though they stumble, they will never fall, for the LORD holds them by the hand" (Ps. 37:24 NLT).

At that moment, Jesus might just recall what he said to Martha, and say it to us: "I am the resurrection and the life. The one who believes in me will live, even though they die; and whoever lives by believing in me will never die" (John 11:25–26).

Then, wiping the tear from his eye, he might ask us as he did her, "Do you believe this?" (v. 26).

I do.

Do you?

PRAYER

You are present, Jesus. And I need you to be. I feel so alone when I consider the one I grieve for. It is so hard to believe when my heart hurts so deeply. I think I believe that you are the resurrection and the life, but help my unbelief. Help me in the ways I doubt and in the ways I think twice. Thank you, Jesus, my resurrection!

FOR REFLECTION

1. Whose death has impacted your life the most?

2. Read John 11:1–44. How does this story give you hope? In what ways is this story also about the ultimate hope we have?

3. What are you mad about? What are you sad about? What are you glad about?

4. When has just being present been all you could do for someone who was grieving? Was there a time when presence was the only gift someone could give you? What impact did that have? How does just being present make an impact when the one who is present is Jesus Christ?

CONCLUSION

THIS TRANSFORMING PRESENCE

The resurrection of Lazarus is not the end of the story in John, of course. But it foreshadows the great resurrection that comes later. It shows that the presence of Jesus so deeply transforms that even death obeys him. This is the ultimate proof that a man was God. John started with this claim: "He was with God in the beginning. Through him all things were made; without him nothing was made that has been made. In him was life, and that life was the light of all mankind" (John 1:2–4). In him was life. Yes, *life*. Not the death that surrounds us.

This transforming presence is why Jesus could gather his disciples before his crucifixion and say, "Do not let your hearts be troubled. . . . If I go and prepare a place for you, I will come back and take you to be with me that you also may be where I am" (14:1, 3). He promised that we will be physically *with* him for all eternity. That is why Jesus prayed, in John 17:24, "Father, I want those you have given me to be with me where I am, and to see my glory, the glory you have given me because you loved me before the creation of the world."

This transforming presence is why Jesus sent us the Holy Spirit after he physically left the earth, so that his Spirit would be *with* us. This is why he could say, "I will ask the Father, and he will give you another advocate to help you and be with you forever—the Spirit of truth. The world cannot accept him, because it neither sees him nor knows him. But you know him, for he lives with you and will be in you" (14:16–17). The Spirit of God is not merely with us, he is in us. Now *that* is a transforming presence.

This transforming presence is why, after Jesus rose from the dead, he spent more time *with* his followers, instructing them of the new kingdom he had ushered in with his crucifixion and resurrection. When the Word became flesh, it truly did change everything.

HAVE YOU BEEN WITH JESUS?

This transforming presence is why, even after Jesus had ascended to heaven, the church exploded in growth and influence and became a world-changing entity, as his body on earth. After Pentecost, the disciples who once trembled in fear at Jesus walking on water were full of boldness, sharing about the transforming presence of Jesus to all those who missed it. Even those who opposed the church and persecuted believers couldn't fail to notice how much the presence of Jesus had changed people: "When they saw the courage of Peter and John and realized that they were unschooled, ordinary men, they were astonished and they took note that these men had been with Jesus" (Acts 4:13).

What might people notice about you because you've been with Jesus? Are they astonished? Do they realize that the presence of God in your life has changed you?

At this question you might feel like the lame man who sat day after day at his post, nothing changing. You might feel like Martha, who felt Jesus showed up too late, or like Nicodemus who was just confused by what Jesus said. When Jesus shows up, it might be when you least expect it. And when he does show up, you might not notice, like at the wedding at Cana. He might even scare the living daylights out of you as he did the disciples in the storm.

Know this: Jesus will show up. He is present. He really is. Believe it. Look for him. The living Son of God is right here with you. And he wants to make all things new for you.

Did you find a character you can relate to in these ten episodes from the book of John? Someone who felt like you feel? Continue to connect with that person or people and consider how you can apply lessons from their lives to your own. Blessed are those who seek Jesus' presence, no matter how they feel.

Are you *exhausted*, like the wedding couple in John 2? Admit that you can't do it on your own and rely on the transforming presence of Jesus to meet your needs, even though you may be unaware he is doing it.

Are you *unsatisfied*, like Nicodemus in John 3? Find your new birth in Jesus by looking to the cross and asking the crucified Christ to satisfy your longings, transforming you and making you new in him.

Are you *trapped*, like the woman at the well in John 4? Only Jesus has the living water you need. Become a true worshiper of the true Messiah so you can offer living water to others who feel trapped as well.

Are you *powerless*, like the royal official in John 4? When you feel in charge but not in control, beg the One who has the power to meet your need. Then believe he can do it.

Are you *stuck*, like the lame man in John 5? Trust your Savior, not your own system, to save you. He is present, so say to the Lord Jesus directly, "I want to be well, and you're the only one who can make it so."

Are you *overwhelmed*, like Andrew in John 6? It all starts by offering your lunch, then watching it multiply when Jesus gets his hands on it. Seek the eternal results only he can supply. Then offer a free lunch to others, along with "food" that saves eternally.

Are you *afraid*, like the disciples in John 6? Remember that Jesus often calms a stormy soul before he calms the storm itself. Take your eyes off the storm and look to the transforming presence of the One who can clear both the storms of your life and clouds of your soul.

Are you *guilty*, like the woman caught in adultery in John 8? Reach your turning point by being truly broken about your sin. Only then can you have a transforming encounter with the God who will not condemn you but empower you to leave your life of sin for a life of joy.

Are you *marginalized*, like the man born blind in John 9? Remember that nobody goes unnamed or unknown in the transforming presence of Jesus Christ. Leave your shame behind, because when others move you to the margins, you are moving closer to Christ.

Are you *grieved*, like Martha in John 11? Believe that our resurrected Savior will one day resurrect us. Express your conviction that Jesus will revive our spirits and restore all things, beginning by resurrecting and transforming our bodies. Believe that he is the resurrection and the life.

Take time in the coming days and months to pray the prayers again from the chapters that apply most directly to your life. Think of these characters as mentors who can influence you through their stories. Remember that they are in the presence of Jesus for all eternity right now. Ask God to reveal your next steps through their lives and situations.

I am also praying that as you continue to read the Bible you will find other people you can relate to. When you open up the Scriptures, may you go beyond reading ideas about God to walking in the shoes of those who encountered the transforming presence of the living Jesus Christ, the Son of God. I pray you will encounter Christ like never before, and in doing so be made new. In each chapter I've provided a prayer for you to pray yourself; now allow me to pray over you as these pages conclude.

PRAYER

You are present, Jesus. Right now, you are present in the place where each reader sits. They believe in you—so you are with them. You cannot be seen, but their faith is even stronger for believing without visual evidence. You are present in such a way that long after they set their book on the shelf, delete it from their reader, give it to a friend, or even discard it, you, Jesus, will still be with them. These are mere words, but you are the Word. They will forget the things I've written. They might even forget the way they felt when they read this. But they won't forget the people they met in Scripture. Each time they hear of these episodes, remind them of your transforming presence. Remind them that they are not alone when they feel the way these people felt. Help them to know that they can truly be made new in you. For you are with us indeed, Jesus. And that changes everything. And you make everything new. Thank you, Jesus, our everything!

NOTES

CHAPTER 2

1. Blaise Pascal, *The Provincial Letters: Moral Teachings of the Jesuit Fathers Opposed to the Church of Rome and Latin Vulgate* (Toronto: William Briggs, 1893), 342.

2. Francis W. Boreham was present for this event at the age of seven. He spoke about the experience in his sermon "Everybody's Text," speaking of the "great granite column, smothered with its maze of hieroglyphics." He watched the relic ascend "from the horizontal to the perpendicular, like a giant waking and standing erect after a long sleep." Stanley Barnes, *Sermons on John 3:16* (Greenville, SC: Ambassador, 1999), 79. Max Lucado has an excellently written description of the Boreham episode in his book *3:16: The Numbers of Hope* (Nashville: Thomas Nelson, 2007).

3. Original source unknown.

4. Billy Graham, interview by Harry Smith, CBS, n.d.

5. A nod here to Ben Witherington, III, *Commentary on John: A Commentary on the Fourth Gospel* (Louisville, Kentucky: Westminster John Knox Press, 1995).

6. U2 (music) and Bono (lyrics), "I Still Haven't Found What I'm Looking For," recorded 1986, on *The Joshua Tree*, Universal, accessed January 12, 2016, http://www.u2.com/lyrics/62.

7. C. S. Lewis, *Mere Christianity* (New York: Macmillan, 1972), 117.

8. Logan Hoffman, "Dad," *Logan Hoffman Writing* (blog), August 19, 2013, http://loganhoffmanwriting.wordpress.com/2013/08/19/dad/.

CHAPTER 3

1. Ben Witherington III, *John's Wisdom: A Commentary on the Fourth Gospel* (Louisville: John Knox Press, 1995), 117.

CHAPTER 4

1. I'm indebted to my colleague Steve DeNeff for the concept of being in charge but not in control, an idea he expressed about King Herod. Steve DeNeff, "When You Are in Charge, but Not in Control" (sermon, College Wesleyan Church, Marion, IN, December 5, 2010).

2. ἠρώτα is used in the imperfect active indicative.

3. Aaron Villa, transcriber, *Willy Wonka and the Chocolate Factory*, last updated February 26, 1999, http://wonkadotcom.tripod.com/script.html.

CHAPTER 5

1. Information compiled from Alistair Jamieson, "Trapped Research Ship, Rescue Vessel Break Free of Antarctic Ice," NBC News, January 8, 2014,

http://worldnews.nbcnews.com/_news/2014/01/08/22222323-trapped-research-ship-rescue-vessel-break-free-of-antarctic-ice; Sandy Fitzgerald, "Antarctic Global Warming Expedition Stuck in Ice for New Year," Newsmax.com, December 31, 2013, http://www.newsmax.com/Newsfront/warming-expedition-stuck-ice/2013/12/31/id/544646/; Rod McGuirk, "Rescue Ship Sent to Retrieve Stranded Antarctic Voyagers Now Stuck in Ice, NBC News, January 3, 2014, http://worldnews.nbcnews.com/_news/2014/01/03/22158911-rescue-ship-sent-to-retrieve-stranded-antarctic-voyagers-now-stuck-in-ice?lite.

CHAPTER 6

1. "Ramesses II," *Wikipedia*, last updated January 7, 2016, https://en.wikipedia.org/wiki/Ramesses_II.

2. Just to note a bit of irony here on the misinterpretation of this legend. In the original "Starfish Thrower" by Loren Eiseley, the story is a bit different and in fact far gloomier. Likewise, the moral of the story is a far more ambivalent and less commercial-ready version of the star thrower we have come to know. Loren Eiseley, "The Star Thrower," in *The Unexpected Universe* (San Diego: Harcourt Brace & Company, 1964), 67–93.

3. Lesslie Newbigin, *The Light Has Come: An Exposition of the Fourth Gospel* (Grand Rapids, MI: Eerdmans, 1982), 78.

CHAPTER 7

1. Chris Hadfield, "How Do You Deal with Fear Versus Danger?," interview with Guy Raz, NPR, TED Radio Hour, May 23, 2014, http://www.npr.org/templates/transcript/transcript.php?storyId=312543097.

2. "STS-111 International Space Station," NASA, last updated November 22, 2007, http://www.nasa.gov/missions/highlights/webcasts/shuttle/sts111/iss-qa.html.

3. "Greek Lexicon: G417 (KJV)," Blue Letter Bible, accessed June 16, 2014, https://www.blueletterbible.org/lang/lexicon/lexicon.cfm?strongs=G417.

4. "Hiking Tips & Wilderness Considerations," Baxter State Park, accessed July 23, 2014, http://www.baxterstateparkauthority.com/hiking/tips.htm.

5. Philip Hoare, "When Whales Attack: The Horrific Truth about Moby-Dick," *The Telegraph*, December 26, 2015, http://www.telegraph.co.uk/film/in-the-heart-of-the-sea/moby-dick-true-story-whales-facts/.

6. "Greek Lexicon: G928 (KJV)," Blue Letter Bible, accessed June 16, 2014, https://www.blueletterbible.org/lang/lexicon/lexicon.cfm?Strongs=G928&t=KJV.

7. "Greek Lexicon: G1719 (KJV)," Blue Letter Bible, accessed June 16, 2014, https://www.blueletterbible.org/lang/lexicon/lexicon.cfm?strongs=G1719.

8. Lesslie Newbigin, *The Light Has Come: An Exposition of the Fourth Gospel* (Grand Rapids, MI: Eerdmans), 76.

9. Ambrose Redmoon, "Ambrose Redmoon," Goodreads.com, accessed January 13, 2016, http://www.goodreads.com/quotes/9809-courage-is-not-the-absence-of-fear-but-rather-the.

10. Samuel Johnson, quoted in Neil T. Anderson and Rich Miller, *Freedom from Fear: Overcoming Worry and Anxiety* (Eugene, OR: Harvest, 1999), 17.

11. Max Lucado, *Fearless: Imagine Your Life without Fear* (Nashville: Thomas Nelson, 2009).

12. For a deeper study into the "do not fear" commands of Christ, seek out these passages: (1) Luke 12:29–32 and Matthew 6:31–33; (2) Mark 5:36 and Luke 8:50; (3) Luke 12:4–5 and Matthew 10:28; (4) Luke 12:6–7 and Matthew 10:29–31; (5) Matthew 24:4–14; Mark 13:5–13; and Luke 21:8–33; (6) John 14:1–4, 6–7, 27; (7) Matthew 17:6; (8) Matthew 28:10; and (9) Luke 5:1–11. For comparison, the eight love commands of Christ are found in Matthew 5:44; 19:19; 22:37, 39; John 13:34; 15:9–10, 12, 17.

CHAPTER 8

1. "Maps of Seven Deadly Sins in America," Memolition: Explore, Dream, Discover, December 12, 2013, http://memolition.com/2013/12/12/maps-of-seven-deadly-sins-in-america/.

2. A. J. Jacobs, *The Year of Living Biblically: One Man's Humble Quest to Follow the Bible as Literally as Possible* (New York: Simon & Schuster, 2007).

3. Beth Brelje, "Once a Bookie for the Mob, Now a Man of God," *Pocono Record*, April 24, 2011, http://www.poconorecord.com/apps/pbcs.dll/article?AID=/20110424/NEWS/110429870/-1/rss01.

4. "Bob Newhart—Stop It!," Realtime Transcription, April 29, 2009, http://www.realtimetranscription.com/showcase/stop_it/.

5. Kasey Musgraves, Brandy Clark, and Shane McAnally, "Follow Your Arrow," recorded 2013, on *Same Trailer Different Park*, Mercury, accessed January 15, 2016, https://play.google.com/music/preview/Ttqxcubupmozk2blpddhl4ap5a4?lyrics=1&utm_source=google&utm_medium=search&utm_campaign=lyrics&pcampaignid=kp-lyrics.

CHAPTER 9

1. Brené Brown, *Daring Greatly: How the Courage to Be Vulnerable Transforms the Way We Live, Love, Parent, and Lead* (New York: Gotham, 2012), 72.

2. Maureen Johnson, *The Madness Underneath: The Shades of London, Book Two* (New York: G. P. Putnam's Sons, 2013), 194.

CHAPTER 10

1. John James Audubon, *Ornithological Biography*, vol. 2 (Edinburgh: Adam & Charles Black, 1834), 321.

2. William Souder, "100 Years after Her Death, Martha, the Last Passenger Pigeon, Still Resonates," *Smithsonian Magazine*, September 2014, http://www.smithsonianmag.com/smithsonian-institution/100-years-after-death-martha-last-passenger-pigeon-still-resonates-180952445/#3JowIr4fLPIfarEl.99.

3. Bible scholars call these the "Imprecatory Psalms." I call them the "Ticked Off at God Psalms." They are Psalms 5, 10, 17, 35, 58–59, 69–70, 79, 83, 109, 129, 137, and 140.

4. Joseph Grenny, "Mastering the Skill of Influence" (lecture, The Global Leadership Summit, Willow Creek Association, South Barrington, IL, August 14–15, 2014).

5. Christopher Hibbert, *Edward VII: The Last Victorian King* (New York: Palgrave Macmillan, 2007), 280.

6. Henry Scott Holland, "The King of Terrors" (sermon, St. Paul's Cathedral, London, May 15, 1910), http://en.wikisource.org/wiki/The_King_of_Terrors. N. T. Wright, in his excellent book, *Surprised by Hope: Rethinking Heaven, the Resurrection, and the Mission of the Church* (New York: HarperCollins, 2008), 13–14, also criticizes this sermon and uses part of the quote I used. Wright shares that the quote is included in the preface of a widely used secular funeral guide.

7. "Revive & Restore," The Long Now Foundation, accessed January 15, 2016, http://longnow.org/revive/.

8. Stewart Brand, "Are We Ready to Hack the Animal Kingdom?," interview with Guy Raz, NPR, TED Radio Hour, last updated July 28, 2015, http://www.npr.org/templates/transcript/transcript.php?storyId=209181592.

9. In order to start a spiritual conversation with a more academic thinker, I've pointed out that a post-apocalyptic scientist might merely think of heaven as the de-extinction lab of the human species, with all of Earth as its museum and habitat.